CW00545769

THE BOROUGH

The Story of Newcastle Borough Police

by

Alf Tunstall

Published by

CHURNET VALLEY BOOKS

43 Bath Street
Leek
Staffordshire
01538 399033

Copyright Alf Tunstall 1995

ISBN 1897949 14 6

Printed in Great Britain by Ipswich Book Co. Ltd., Ipswich, Suffolk.

All rights reserved. No part of this publication may be reproduced,
stored in a retrieval system or transmitted, in any form or by any
means, electronic, mechanical, photocopying, recording or otherwise,
without the prior permission of the author and publisher in writing.

Acknowledgments

I would like to thank the following without whose help this book would not have been possible.

I must say a special thank you to Jeff Cowdell, who spent many hours deciphering my illegible handwriting and typing out the draft copy. Also to Mr Peter Wilkinson of the Newcastle Museum for his help and encouragement.

I am also most grateful to the following for their help and advice in the preparation of this history.

Sergeant Alan Walker, Police Headquarters, Stafford
The staff at the Newcastle Public Library reference dept.
Ex Chief Superintendent R Hazell
Ex Superintendent CR Lester
Mrs Audrey Gleves
Mr John Naylor
Mrs E Chadwick
Miss P Skinner
Mrs B Cummings
Mrs L Berry
Mr John Lightfoot

*This book is dedicated to the memory of
ex Chief Superintendent Raymond Hazell who was
a perfect gentleman. He unfortunately did not live
to see its publication, dying a few weeks ago.*

Newcastle Borough Police 1920

Left to right;
P C Hawley, Sgt Connolly, Sgt Black, ---, George Moundsey, Alan Williams, George Swettenham

INTRODUCTION

The New Police

The first paid, professional police force in England was established in 1829 by Sir Robert Peel, the then Home Secretary, when he formed the Metropolitan Police Force in London.

The New Police, as they were known, soon became so successful in London that the criminals soon began to move out to the smaller provincial towns. To combat this growing problem, some of the towns decided to set up police forces of their own, along similar lines to London. Newcastle-under-Lyme was one of them. Only a few months after the force had been formed, the government passed the Municipal Corporations Act of 1835. This act compelled all boroughs to set up a watch committee and appoint a head constable and other constables.

The County and Borough Police Act of 1856 had a far reaching effect on all police forces. It compelled every county that had not already done so to set up a paid professional police force. It also appointed government inspectors, known as Her Majesty's Inspectors of Constabulary. They were to inspect every police force annually and, if the force came up to government standard and was certified efficient, the government would pay one quarter of the cost of pay and clothing. Later, in 1874, this was raised to half the cost of pay and clothing. A few years later the government decided to fund half the total cost of all forces which were found to be efficient.

Newcastle was to lose its own Borough force on 1st April 1947 when, along with 44 other non-county borough forces in England and Wales, it was merged with its respective county, so ending the 113 years of service which the force had given to the people of the Borough.

It is now almost fifty years since the Newcastle Borough Force ceased to exist as a separate entity, and this seems an apt moment in time to record this history for the few members of the Borough Force who are still left - some of whom I knew - and for posterity.

Alf Tunstall

Newcastle-under-Lyme Borough Police
Winners of the North Staffordshire Ambulance Cup, 23rd July, 1904.
Back: Dr Allardice, Chief Constable George Ingram, Mr S Wade, Secretary, NSR Co.
Front: PC C V Gillies, PC H Watkins, PC T Rawlinson, PC J C Morgan.   *Miss Ingram*

Newcastle-under-Lyme Borough Police, decorated truncheon, early issue.
Courtesy of Inspector David Baldwin.

THE BOROUGH MEN

**The Early Days
1834 - 1839**

The seeds for the establishment of a full time professional police force in the Borough were first sown at a meeting of the Watch Committee, held in the Guildhall at Newcastle on 1st November 1834. At this meeting it was decided to appoint a sufficient number of men to act by day and by night as constables in the said Borough.

Isaac Cottrill was appointed Chief Officer at a salary of £150 per annum. George Coomer and Charles Woolley were appointed Assistant Constables at £1 per week. Uniforms were provided and a stove was provided for the Constable's Room at a cost of three shillings. Later that year the Constables were issued with top hats. The first bill presented by Isaac Cottrill to the Watch Committee was for the sum of £4.7s.7d. for stationery.

In May 1839, both Constables quit their posts and were replaced by John Stanway and James Booth. By April 1840 John Stanway had resigned and was replaced by Charles Bloor.

**Chartists Riots
1842**

During 1842, most of the Potteries towns were in the grip of Chartist riots. Police lock-ups came under attack and many were burnt down. Vicarages and public houses were looted. When the rioters had finished sacking and burning the Potteries towns, they advanced towards Newcastle. News of their impending arrival had already reached the town and the Mayor and Chief Constable made their plans.

A force of 800 Special Constables was quickly assembled and two cannons were place outside the Police Office. The Chief Constable then obtained the services of a soldier in full uniform, who happened to be on leave in the town. He organised the loan of a musket and then took the soldier to the Borough boundary at the top of George Street, where a barricade was hastily constructed across the road. The Chief Constable stood behind the barricade and ordered the soldier to parade on the Stoke side with his musket, as if on guard.

The approaching mob saw the soldier, assumed that the Militia were ready and waiting and turned round without ever entering Newcastle. In recognition of his action the Chief Constable was presented with a gold watch and a purse of 100 guineas from the Duke of Sutherland and the grateful townsfolk. Mr Lester, the Mayor, had a number of cutlasses manufactured, the blades of which were inscribed **"W.O.Lester, Mayor 1842"** and on the reverse side **"Newcastle under Lyme Borough Police"**. These cutlasses were placed in the Police Office as a precaution against further riots!

First Talk of Amalgamation

As a direct result of the 1842 Chartist riots, the Staffordshire County Constabulary was established. At the same time, a proposal was made to amalgamate the small Borough force with the new Constabulary, but two petitions objecting to the merger were received and the amalgamation did not take place.

Dismissal of the Chief Constable 1849

However, all was not well with the Borough force. Its Chief Constable, Isaac Cottrill, had a liking for strong drink which had, on more than one occasion, been the reason for his absence from duty. Things came to a head in 1849 when it was discovered that, for the previous twelve years he had been misappropriating funds allocated for the fire brigade. Cottrill was dismissed from office in December 1849. Even the gift of 100 guineas, which he had received

earlier in his service, was withdrawn. Prior to his appointment to Newcastle, Isaac Cottrill had been a Superintendent of Police at Pendleton, Lancashire.

The uniform of the Borough Police at this period was modelled on that worn by the Metropolitan Police and is described as blue with white buttons and embroidery.

Following the dismissal of Cottrill, the Watch Committee received 43 applications for the vacant post. A short list was drawn up and the following three people were interviewed:
Police Sergeant T Steer, Metropolitan Police
Superintendent JT Blood, Staffordshire Constabulary
Superintendent S Harlow Monmouthshire Police

Chief Constable J T Blood 1850 - 1855

On 7th February 1850, Superintendent JT Blood who had been in charge of the Uttoxeter Division of the County force was appointed as Cottrill's successor.
The Watch Committee drew up a list of rules and regulations to be closely monitored. They did not want any repetition of the Cottrill affair!

Probable dress at this time modelled on Metropolitan Police

At this time the Chief Constable was give permission to grant 24 hours leave of absence, but any leave in excess of that had to be agreed by the Mayor and two justices.

It was said of Chief Constable Blood that he was too much the bureaucrat and it was difficult to entice him out of his Police Office. Blood always maintained that his time in the office was inevitable because of the illiteracy of his constables. The Council resolved to give him more assistance in the office to enable him to spend more time in town and the force was increased by one man - John Pipper was appointed on 22nd November 1851 at the rate of 18 shillings per week. Less than a month later he resigned!

The Watch Committee decidedat this point to hold an inquiry into the efficiency of the force. The Chief Constable said that PC Bloor was a most efficient officer and a good detective, but would be better if he were a stranger to the town. *"I believe that policemen should be strangers to the town. I urge you not to replace Pipper with a local man."*
Pipper was replaced by a Mr Pendograss but from whence he came is not recorded. In 1854, one further constable was added to the strength with the appointment of George Morrow.

Early discipline problems 1854

In January 1854, PC Pendograss tendered his resignation. When called before the committee and asked for the reason, he said that PC Bloor had been circulating false reports about him and had rendered his situation uncomfortable. PC Bloor was called before the committee and asked to explain himself. He was then ordered to resign. The Watch Committee instructed the Town Clerk to insert the necessary advertisement in the usual papers.

In April, Bloor was called before the committee again and his resignation was rescinded, but he was warned as to his future conduct. A new constable, William Knott was appointed at this time and a boot allowance of five shillings per year was allowed.

Chief Constable Blood tended his resignation to the committee in 1855. Speaking on behalf of the committee, the Mayor told him,

"We are sorry to lose you, you have been a very able officer and carried out your duties in a most satisfactory manner since your appointment in 1850."

At Mr Blood's request, the Council purchased all the fittings in his house at a cost of £9.9s.0d.

The usual advertisement was placed in the newspapers and the following four persons interviewed:

Charles Barnes   Superintendent of Police, Birkenhead, Lancashire & Cheshire Joint Railway.

George Clayton   Sub Inspector, Staffordshire Constabulary stationed at Burslem.

William Bostock Nottingham County Constabulary.

Charles Bailey   Inspector, Staffordshire Constabulary, stationed at Stoke.

Chief Constable Charles Barnes 1855 - 1857

Charles Barnes was the successful candidate. His pay was £90 per annum with a free house, coal and gas but this was considerably less than the first Chief Constable, who had been paid £150 per annum. Mr Barnes was allowed travelling expenses of £1.10s.0d. A few days after the appointment of Charles Barnes, PC Knott was ordered to resign, having made a false report about the new Chief Constable.

On 28th December 1856, Thomas Lawley of Wellington, Shropshire, was appointed as a police constable at 20 shillings per week. However after only three months service, PC Lawley decided that a policeman's life was not for him and resigned in March 1857. In the same month six pairs of handcuffs were purchased and new capes and overshoes issued.

PC Charles Smith of the County Police from Hartshill was appointed to replace Lawley. The Town Clerk was instructed to write to Mr Hatton, Chief Constable of the County of Stafford, regarding his testimonials. It was then discovered that Smith had been dismissed from the County force when allegations had been made against him by a person named Thomas Langley. When the full committee had studied the letter it was decided that Smith should be allowed to continue as a constable with the Borough. Not for long however. He was dismissed three months later for using abusive and using insulting language to the Mayor. On the day of his dismissal, a PC Movion also resigned.

The Sir George Gray Police Bill 1856

In November 1856, at a meeting of the Watch Committee, the Sir George Grey Police Bill was discussed but the committee decided to take no action. The Town Clerk was instructed to write to Chief Superintendent Sweeting in charge of the County Constabulary for the Potteries Division and ask on what evidence he had based the following statements put before the Government Commissioners inquiry into local government in the Potteries:

> 1. That up to 300 rag and bone gatherers leave Newcastle every morning to travel into the Potteries.

> 2. What grounds he has for stating that they can be dealt with in Tunstall more efficiently by his policemen than in the Borough.

> 3. Why the Borough jurisdiction hinders him in his duty.

The Town Clerk was also to write to the Government Commissioner about the statement.

At this time, a PC Mitchell resigned and a PC Phillips of Uttoxeter was appointed to replace him.

On 12th December, the Watch Committee ordered that a die be cast for the Police buttons and new uniforms and hats were to be purchased at 12 shillings each.

PC Lovelock resigned. Approval was granted for an additional constable so advertisements were placed in the newspapers for two Constables at 17 shillings each per week. William Lewis of Wolstanton and a Charles Wardell were appointed.

A letter was received from Captain Bricknell, Chief Constable of Lincolnshire, saying that Superintendent Barnes had applied for a position in that Force and requesting information. Barnes had apparently applied for this post without the knowledge of the committee. He was called before the committee and dismissed. But Alderman Phillips said that his dismissal should be reconsidered because he would not be able to take any Police jobs again. The committee rescinded the dismissal and asked Mr Barnes to resign.

Advertisement for New Superintendent 1857

In April 1857, the Watch Committee had the following advertisement placed in a number of newspapers:

WANTED - a steady, active and intelligent man possessing the necessary qualifications to superintend the Police of the Borough of Newcastle-under-Lyme. He will have the assistance of four active Constables in constant pay.
The inspection of the Weights and Measures and Lodging houses and of Markets and Fairs also the

direction of the Fire Brigade are to be attended to by the Superintendent.
He will be allowed a house rent free and clear of local rates, also coal for firing, gas lighting and water rent and a salary of £90 per annum.

In view of what had occurred with Mr Barnes, the Watch Committee passed the following regulation -
"the Chief Constable or any constable of this Borough will not seek employment with any other police force without first obtaining the permission of the Watch Committee."

**Chief Constable
Mr Charles Booth
1857 - 1861**

There were quite a number of replies to the advertisement for the vacant post of Chief Constable but after studying the applications, the job was offered to Mr Charles Booth. He was an ex-Alderman of the Borough but had no previous police experience.

In July 1857, PC Charles Bloor applied for an increase in pay. He was granted an increase of one shilling per week, in view of his long service. He had been a member of the force for seventeen years.

At the July Watch Committee, PCs Wardell and Phillips were not so lucky. Wardell was reprimanded for being drunk on duty on two occasions and PC Phillips was dismissed for committing the same offence on several occasions. One month later PC Wardell resigned.

PC Lewis was granted a pay increase to 19 shillings per week.

There were now two vacancies to be filled. In September 1858 John Garson and Henry Eardley were appointed at 19 shillings each per week.

Inspection of the Borough Police. Force Declared Inefficient! 1858

At the end of 1858, Her Majesty's Inspector of Constabulary, Major General Cartwright, inspected the force and said that the Borough police force was inefficient through weakness in strength, with only one Chief Constable and four Constables to a population in excess of 11,000. This meant that there would be no grant from the Home Office!

With only a few weeks service, PC Henry Eardley was asked to resign when it was said that he had been on sick leave for five weeks and Dr Woods said that he would not be fit for duty for some time yet. The committee agreed to pay the doctor's fee of one guinea. PC George Chidley was appointed as a replacement.

The Chief Constable was granted an increase in pay of £10 per annum. This brought his pay up to £100 per annum, still £50 less than Chief Constable Cottrill was paid when he was appointed. At this time, a letter was received from the Home Office to say that, in future, the Chief Officers of all borough forces would be titled Chief Superintendent and not Chief Constable.

Amalgamation Discussed again 1858

During the last week of 1858, a Watch Committee meeting was held at which the amalgamation of the Borough force with the County was discussed yet again.

At the same time a William Lea was appointed to the force. Less than six months later PC Lea was called before the Watch Committee to answer allegations made against him by Sylvia Morwood that he had indecently assaulted her. He was warned about his future conduct!

Chief Constable Mr Booth asked to Resign! 1861

In 1861 an application was received from the Chief Constable and constables asking for an increase in pay. But instead, the Watch Committee asked Chief Constable Mr Booth to resign because they claimed that his conduct had been unsatisfactory on several counts.

The pay increase for the constables would not be entertained either.

Chief Constable Mr Williams 1861 - 1866

So the Watch Committee had to advertise yet again for a replacement. Inspector Williams of Silverdale and Sergeant Vernon Carroll of Stafford, both of the County Police were called before the Watch Committee for interview. Inspector Williams was appointed. Sergeant Vernon Carroll was paid £1 in expenses. When Mr Williams took charge of the Borough force, the total strength was six men to a population of 12,600. Soon after, PC Bloor, who had been a member of the force for over twenty years was promoted to Sergeant in recognition of his long service.

At the request of the Chief Constable, the Fire Brigade was reorganised and an advert for candidates was displayed in front of the Police Office.

Home Office Scheme Turned Down 1862

In September 1862, the Mayor received a letter from the Home Office requesting details of a superannuation fund and asking that a sufficient number of men be appointed to allow the Borough to participate in the Home Office Scheme, which would, in their opinion, be beneficial to the Borough. It was decided that no action would be taken on either count as the Mayor said that it would involve the appointment of seven additional men. In the end, it was agreed to appoint two extra men. These were Mr Pegg and Mr Fox, both residents of the Borough.

A few months after his appointment, it came to light that PC Pegg had been fined by the County magistrates at Hanley for assault upon a soldier at a beer house in Etruria. He was called before the Watch Committee and reprimanded and ordered to forego one shilling per week from his pay for three months.

Seven day working for PCs 1864

The Watch Committee decided that, with effect from 29th April 1864, the whole of the police force would be on duty from 3pm to 10pm on Sundays until further notice.

PC Pegg was reprimanded for being drunk and absent from duty from 10.20pm to 11.30pm and PC Fox was ordered to be more efficient in his duties.

In June 1864 both PC Fox and Sergeant Bloor handed their resignations to the Watch Committee.

Sergeant Bloor had completed over 24 years of service. He was presented with £5 by the Watch Committee in consideration of his long service. There was no superannuation fund in existence of course in the Borough force at that time.

In the same month Samuel Myott and Henry Mitchell were appointed as constables. PC Lea was promoted to sergeant in place of Mr Bloor. In July, with only one month behind him PC Mitchell was fined 2/6d and reprimanded for being drunk on duty. At the same meeting of the Watch Committee PC Chidley was in trouble for being absent from his point at 11.15pm on the 16th inst. and 12.45pm on the17th inst. and using language, unbecoming of a police officer to the sergeant. He was ordered to show more respect to his senior officers and fined 2/6d.

Sergeant Bloor was ordered to send into the office his last issue of clothing with the exception of his stripes and crown!

Government Inspection and Increase in Establishment 1864

In September 1864, the Government Inspector's report was read before the committee in which he suggested the following strength of force:

One Superintendent	@ £90 per annum
One Sergeant	@ 23/- per week
One Act Sergeant	@ 21/- per week
4 1st Class Constables	@ 20/- per week
5 2nd Class Constables	@ 18/- per week
12 Officers in total.	

Cost of the Pay and Clothing	£718. 8s. 0d
Less 25% grant from Home Office	£179.12s.0d
Cost to the Borough	£538.12s.0d

This he proposed, would bring the force up to efficiency. The scheme was considered and rejected. It was decided that there would be no need to increase the number of constables!

At the first Watch Committee Meeting in 1865, PC Mitchell was again fined, this time 8 shillings for being drunk on duty, the fine to be paid at the rate of one shilling per week for eight weeks.

The Chief Constable also reported that he and PC Chidley had a case of trespass bought against them by a Thomas Jeremiah Head, an officer of the County forces, resulting in the County Court Judge verdict in favour of the plaintiff for £5. The committee said the damages were excessive but agreed to pay all costs and a cheque for £9.4s.6d. was sent. It was resolved that:

"in the opinion of the committee the damages given in the said action were excessive and unwarranted by the fact of the case that the plaintiff's conduct as a police officer of the County was highly answerable, as amounting to aiding and assisting of a person convicted of an assault from being taken upon a warrant of commitment issued by the Magistrates of this Borough."

It is fascinating to speculate the circumstances in which an arrest by one police force was obstructed by another!

HM Inspector's Report Superannuation Fund Started 1865

In September 1865, the Government Inspector of the Constabulary said that the force was still inefficient due to the weakness in numbers. The Watch Committee decided to set up a superannuation fund and to employ four additional constables. By October the following men had been sworn in as constables:

> John Burke of Earl Street, Newcastle.
> James Hissey of Harrison Street, Newcastle
> William Benton of Goose Street, Newcastle
> Frederick Dutton of 27 Newtown, Stafford

At the end of the year, tenders were issued to Mr Alfred Thomas Taylor of Bridge Street, Newcastle for uniforms for the following 12 months. The cost was:

Top coats	£2. 4s.0d each
Trousers	19s.0d per pair
Hats	10s.6d each
Frock coats and trousers together	£3.10s.0d

It was also agreed that two pairs of trousers per year would be issued.

In November 1865, the Chief Constable had a pay increase of £10 per annum bringing his pay up to £100 per annum and all other members of the force had an increase in pay to the recommended level set by the HM Inspector of Constabulary.

At the last meeting of the Watch Committee for 1865, PC Hissey, who had only been a member of the force for a few weeks, was required to resign when he was charged with being absent from duty. It was said that he had enlisted in the 52nd Regiment of Foot. To replace Hissey, a PC Marriott was appointed, who produced testimonials from the County Police.

P Cs Accused of Drunkenness again 1866

On January 16th 1866 PCs Myott and Pegg were found drinking together in the Shakespeare Public House in George Street, when they should have been on duty. Each was given a 5 shillings fine.

In January, the committee was to supply, at the recommendation of the Chief Constable, arm bands to be worn by every constable when on duty. It is not known, however, if such bands were ever worn.

In April 1866 PC Mitchell made his final appearance before the Watch Committee to answer the charge that he had been found drinking in the Three Horseshoes public house at 2.30pm when he should have been on duty. He was ordered to resign. PC Mitchell was replaced by a Joseph Vigrass who again did not stay for long - he was dismissed in September for officiating at an illegal barefist prize fight.

The pay for a constable was now 20/-. Sergeant Lee tendered his resignation. He had been in the force since 1858 and a sergeant from 1864 - long service at this time - and was thanked by the committee and given a gratuity of £5 for his good conduct. PC Chidley was promoted to sergeant.

Chief Constable Stanford Alexander 1866 - 1870

Mr Williams the Chief Constable resigned along with PC Myott. Advertisements were placed in the Staffordshire Advertiser, the Staffordshire Sentinel and the Birmingham Post. Thirteen applications were received and a Mr Stanford Alexander was elected unanimously. He had held posts with both the Birmingham Police and the Leominster Borough Police previously. He brought with him PC Bretherstone who became sergeant on the force with Sergeant Chidley.

New Helmets 1866

At the end of 1866, a new type of helmet was issued to replace the silk hats that had been worn up to that time, but it appears they were unpopular with the men. A few months later they contacted the Watch Committee, requesting that they be allowed to wear silk hats in the day and use the helmets only at night. The committee agreed. From photographs of the time, it appears that these helmets were of the shako type and not helmets in the modern sense. In 1869, they were again issued to the force, as it was pointed out by the committee that the silk hats cost 8/9d each against 7/6d for a helmet. It was also at this time that metal numbers were first attached to the uniform and 1st Class Constables were given a mark to wear on their arm - this at the recommendation of Her Majesty's Inspector.

In December 1866, PC Marriott was promoted to the rank of sergeant. He had only been a member of the force for a few months but he had been a County constable prior to this. Three more members appointed to the force in 1866 were Moses Moyan of Hatton, William Lloyd and William Carter, both of Newcastle. Found asleep on duty, PC Benton was reprimanded by the Mayor. He was later fined 2/6 for being drunk on duty.

Thomas Whitehurst of Sandon and Henry Banks of Hanley, both County constables were appointed to the force to replace PCs Myott and Mitchell.

Discipline Problems Continue

The Chief Constable reported PC Burke for Neglect of Duty: He had been sent with two prisoners to Stafford. When he returned he did not report himself for duty - the train had left Stafford at 10.20 and he should have been back for 2.00pm. He did not report for duty until 10.00pm and then was found 2 hours later by

Sergeant Chidley drinking in a pub.
He was ordered to resign!

**More Discipline
Problems
1867**

At the first meeting of the Watch Committee in 1867, PC
Whitehurst was reprimanded for being drunk on duty. James
Hammersley, who had previously served with the Poole Borough
force was appointed to the force. He was to serve less than 12
months for in April he was reported for being drunk on duty, using
bad language to the Sergeant and losing his helmet. In November
he was before the Watch Committee again on a charge of drinking
on duty and this time there was no reprimand - he was dismissed!

The Chief Constable was allowed an increase for prisoners' meals
from 8d to one shilling per day.
In October 1867 PC Dutton resigned, having been in the force for
two years. Daniel Wheat of Wolstanton was appointed to fill the
vacancy. John Deakin, a groom at the Stoke Workhouse, was also
appointed to replace PC Hammersley.
The Chief Constable's pay was increased by £15 per annum.

**Sergeant Chidley
Sued for Assault on
Woman**

In January 1868, Mr John Gibbons took action in the County
Court against Sergeant Chidley for assault upon his wife. He
was awarded £8.12s.6d against the sergeant.
When all the facts of the case were made
known to the Watch Committee they agreed to
pay all the sergeant's costs from the Borough
fund.

**Drink and
DisciplineProblems
again
1868**

PCs Pegg and Benton were also in trouble in
February 1868, for improper conduct. It was
reported that between 3 and 4 am they had
brought a stranger into the Police Office and at
his request and expense purchased a quantity
of whisky from the Albion and that Pegg and
Benton stayed with him in the office drinking.
They were both reprimanded and all the other
officers were cautioned about committing
similar offences in future.
PC Lewis, who had been a member of the force since 1857, was
awarded £20 from the superannuation fund when it was reported

that he had been off sick for quite a long time and that the doctor did not think that he would be fit to resume police duty again.

Sergeants Chidley and Marriott requested an increase in pay but this was rejected by the committee.

Thomas Harrison of Ashbourne, Derbyshire and a Mr Carter and Eli Bentley of Newcastle were sworn in as members of the force at the end of December 1868.

More Discipline Problems 1869

The new year was only a few days old when PC Benton was up before the committee yet again, this time for being drunk when giving evidence before the Recorder at Quarter Sessions! His pay was reduced by one shilling per week. PC Carter, who had only been in the force a few weeks, resigned. The vacancy was filled by Frederick Dutton, who applied for his old job again, having resigned in October 1867.

In September, James Morgan was appointed to the force, having previously been employed as a warder at Millbank Prison. But in February of the following year, he was reported to the committee by the Chief Constable for four offences, three for Neglect of Duty and the fourth for *"having connections with a prostitute, Hannah Edwards, on Sunday in an entry in Penkhull Street"*. The Neglect of Duty charges had not been put into the Discipline Book until several days after the alleged offences and could not be proven. For the fourth offence he was warned to be more careful in future. He resigned a few weeks later!

Resignation of Chief Constable Mr Alexander 1870

On 21st September 1870, the Chief Constable tendered his resignation, along with PCs William Lloyd and Gittings. They were not to lose contact with North Staffordshire, for they travelled only two miles up the road, to become members of the recently formed Hanley Borough Police force - Mr Alexander in fact becoming its first Chief Constable. PC Lloyd later moved on to become Chief Constable of Louth Borough Police in Lincolnshire.

Chief Constable Mr Walter Jones 1870 - 1877

Four applicants were shortlisted for the vacant post of Chief Constable:

William Harris   Inspector of Nuisances, Birmingham

Inspector Carswell	Sheffield Police
Inspector Jones	Salford Police
Sergeant Marriott	Newcastle-under-Lyme Police

Sergeant Marriott later withdrew his application and the successful applicant was Inspector Jones from Salford Police, who took sixteen of the seventeen votes. Sergeant Marriott's and Sergeant Chidley's pay was raised by one shilling per week.

The two vacancies in the force were filled by Robert Hunter of Pendleton Lancashire and John Mandley of Newcastle. Mr T Cook of Congleton Cheshire was allowed £1 out of the Borough fund towards travelling costs for attending the interviews.

The Town Clerk was told to ask for tenders in a number of newspapers for uniform, including military style caps and helmets.

In November 1870 the Mayor received a letter from the Home Office requesting information about the treatment of a Richard Hughes, a lunatic who had been locked up in the police station cells (we presume questioning such incarceration).

In the same month, PC Pegg and a newcomer, PC Hunter were reported for that most common of offences in this period - Drunk on Duty - both received warnings about their conduct.

At the beginning of 1871 the policemen were issued with capes, the cost of which was 10/9d each.

PC Unwin was fined 10/- for being drunk on duty and PC Harrison, who had been a member of the force since 1868, resigned. His place was filled by Joseph Harvey. In June both Sergeants and all Constables were awarded a pay increase of 1/- per week.

Sergeant Chidley Fined by Magistrates 1871

In August 1871, Sergeant Chidley appeared before the local Magistrate's Court. It was alleged that he had been on duty and drinking at the Alma Inn in George Street Newcastle and that he had assaulted one Richard Cliffe with a stick causing bodily harm. Chidley was fined forty shillings or one month's imprisonment. He was later reprimanded by the Mayor and told that if anything like this happened again he would be dismissed!

In October 1871 PCs Mandley, Benton and Harvey were before the committee to answer a charge of drunk on duty. PC Harvey was asked to resign, the case against PC Benton was not substantiated and PC Mandley, who also had the additional charge against him of using abusive language to the Chief Constable, was told that if he was reported again he would be dismissed.

Her Majesty's Inspector of Constabulary reports again 1871

Her Majesty's Inspector of Constabulary laid his report before the Watch Committee at the end of 1871. He said that the population of the Borough was 15,949 and there should be one constable to every 1000 head of population. The committee said that they were willing to increase the establishment to 14 men - we hope this will be sufficient. The Town Clerk was asked to write to the County authorities asking about the terms for an amalgamation of the Borough forces with the County. The Borough force was twelve strong at that time.

The Chief Constable reported that there had been 209 cases of drunkenness in the Borough in 1870 and 338 cases in 1871. The Watch Committee must have taken pity on the Chief Constable's increased workload because at the same meeting he was awarded a pay rise of £10 per annum.

The force was increased by the addition of two men at the beginning of 1872. Sergeant Marriott resigned due to sickness and was awarded a gratuity of £50 from the superannuation fund. PC Pegg was promoted to Sergeant in Marriott's place. The promotion, however, did not bring him much luck because in the June he died of smallpox and typhoid fever! His widow received £52.10s.0d from the superannuation fund. PC Dutton was promoted to fill the vacancy left by Pegg's death. Dutton had joined the force for the second time in 1869. PC Wheat was

promoted to Merit Class. At this time military caps were purchased at a cost of 4/- each and issued to members of the force.

In the month of May PC Mandley was before the Watch Committee again. He was said to have assisted two county court bailiffs in taking furniture from the home of Mr Michael Gill and handcuffing him and bringing him to the Police Office on a false charge, when he was off duty. He was also charged with being insolent to the Chief Constable. PC Mandley, in return, also brought a charge against the Chief Constable for assault in connection with the above incident. PC Mandley was warned by the committee about his future conduct. The Chief Constable was also told that he had exceeded his duty in striking Mandley!

HM Inspector and Watch Committee Disagree 1872

In September of 1872, the Watch Committee had a meeting with Colonel Cobb, Her Majesty's Inspector of Constabulary for the Midlands. The Colonel said that the force was still inefficient due to lack of manpower and should be increased to fifteen men. The committee later took a vote on this and the motion was lost by 4 votes to 6. Councillor Robinson said that the force should be decreased to nine men, including the Chief Constable. A vote was taken on this and it was agreed to reduce the force to nine men. At the same meeting the Watch Committee agreed to pay PC Wheat £10 in respect of services he had performed in the recent smallpox outbreak.

Force reduced to Nine Men 1873

In January 1873, the Chief Constable reported to the committee that he had reduced the force to nine men as instructed and was now unable to work the force efficiently with that number of men!

Drunkenness and Insubordination Continue

In the same month poor old PC Benton was in trouble yet again when he was reported for being drunk on duty and taking the Mayor into custody on a groundless charge. PC Benton was later cleared of all charges.
PC Mandley was fined 2/6d for being unfit for duty due to drink. Only fourteen days later, PC Benton made yet another appearance, this time the charge was drunk and disorderly and use of indecent and insubordinate language to the Chief Constable. He was fined £1 and ordered to apologise to the Chief Constable.

Watch Committee Complies with Inspector 1874

At the end of January the Watch Committee decided after all to comply with the report of the Inspector of Constabulary and increase the force to 15 men.

At the end of the year Sergeant Chidley's pay was increased to thirty shillings per week.

With effect from May 1874, two police officers would in future be stationed at the Butts Rifle Range when the Staffordshire Volunteers were camping. The Watch Committee decided to issue the Chief Constable with a uniform suit.

The Mayor said they had received a letter from the Home Office saying that the post of Inspector of Nuisances was no longer to be carried out by the police.

At this time an application was received from the constables for a pay increase. The committee ordered the Chief Constable to write to other Boroughs of a similar size to inquire what they paid their policemen.

Sergeant Chidley & PC Braithwaite Dismissed 1874

At the July meeting of the Watch Committee the Chief Constable read our the following:

"I have reported Sergeant Chidley for neglect of duty and PC Braithwaite for gross neglect of duty. The facts are that PC Braithwaite had allowed one Sara Stacey, a servant girl employed by Mr Howson of King Street, Newcastle, to accompany him on his beat from 11pm until 1.20am on the nights of 23,24,25,26, unknown to Mr Howson and that he had committed an act of criminal assault on Sara Stacey on the night of the 24th, by damaging her dress and she had now been dismissed from her situation."

The sergeant had also failed to report PC Braithwaite and PC Deakin for being drunk on the morning of the 13th and failing to visit the other night constable for two hours previous to finishing duty. Both Sergeant Chidley and PC Braithwaite were dismissed. Chidley had been a member of the force since 1859 and had been promoted to sergeant in 1866. It might be said that he had had an eventful service!

Sergeant Dutton was promoted to 1st Class Sergeant and PC Blyth to Sergeant and three further men were appointed to the force, so for the first time in its history, the Borough force was up to its establishment figure of fifteen officers.

More Dismissals for Indiscipline 1874

In December of 1874 PC Benton's luck also finally ran out. He was ordered to resign from the force for using obscene language and insubordination to the night sergeant.

The order was placed in 1875 for the following items of uniform;

15 Blue frock coats and trousers @ £3 3s. 6d. each	
15 pairs trousers @	£1 11s. 6d. each
16 Great coats @	£2 11s. 6d. each
14 Capes @	13s. 6d. each
14 Helmets @	9s. 6d. each

Early Juvenile Deliquents! 1875

John Bickerton, Robert Dower and John Cartlidge were appointed to the force and the Chief Constable's pay was increased to £140 per annum. Constables were ordered to keep watch and pay regular visits to the gymnasium as part of their beat, as youths had been causing damage.

PC Weaver reported Sergeant Deakin for making a false entry in his report of the night of 11th December. Weaver said that at 4.30am on the night in question, Sergeant Deakin and himself were drinking in the King's Brewery with Mr D Smith and H Hill, two employees of the brewery. The Chief Constable was told to contact Smith and Hill and request that they attend the next meeting of the Watch Committee. The allegations were found to be false and PC Weaver was asked for his resignation.

PC Unwin was ordered to take one month's unpaid leave for being found drunk on duty again.

Both sergeants were to be paid at the same rate of 30 shillings per week.

First Probationary Constable 1877

In March 1877, Bernard Plant was appointed a probationary constable. This is the first time that anyone is mentioned in the Watch Committee records as a probationary constable. All appointments to the force after this date would appear to be on probation.

A portrait of Isaac Cottrill, painted shortly before he was dismissed from his position as Chief Officer of Police. Cottrill established the Borough Police force in 1834 and staunchly defended the town against the Chartists in 1842.

The first known photograph of the Borough Police Force, taken c1888.   *Author's collection*

**Good Report from
HM Inspector
1877**

Her Majesty's Inspector issued his report into the force and said that all was efficient. The only suggestion he had was that the boot allowance be increased - from fourpence halfpenny per week to seven pence! At the September meeting of the Watch Committee, the Chief Constable read out a request from the constables and sergeants, to be allowed one day off duty per month. The Chief Constable was instructed to write to Lichfield and other boroughs of the same size to ascertain the situation in these forces and report back to the Watch Committee. At the same meeting the Chief Constable was made Inspector of Explosives!

**Dismissal of Chief
Constable Jones
1877**

In December 1877 the School Board wrote to the Watch Committee complaining about the conduct of the Chief Constable, claiming that he had failed to collect all the fines imposed by the magistrates for non-attendance at school. The board revealed that quite a number were still outstanding. This was only the start of the the Chief Constable's problems. Two months later he was sent for by the Watch Committee and told they were not happy as he had absented himself from duty for a longer period than he had been granted by the Mayor. Neither the council nor the Watch Committee had any confidence in him. The committee ordered that all books and documents be removed from the Police Office and placed in the care of the Mayor. The Chief Constable was dismissed from office and Sergeant Blyth was appointed to take charge of the force on a temporary basis.

**Chief Constable
Mr Blyth
1877 - 1881**

The committee decided not to advertise for a successor to Mr Jones, but instead to offer the vacant post to Sergeant Blyth. Some members thought the job should be given to Sergeant Dutton, so it was decided to put the matter to the vote, and each man received eleven votes. The meeting was adjourned and the Town Clerk was asked to advise. A second vote was taken and this time Blyth gained eleven votes to Dutton's ten, with one abstention, and became the eighth Chief Constable since 1834. PC Swinwood was promoted to fill the vacancy created by Sergeant Blyth's promotion.

The Chief Constable was paid £120 per year at this time, while the sergeant's pay was thirty shillings per week. Constables on appointment were paid 21/- per week, 2nd Class 23/- per week and

1st Class 25/- per week. The new Chief Constable suggested that new serge jackets and military caps be issued.

It was recommended to the committee that PC Unwin be asked to resign as it was said that he was suffering from infirmity of the mind. He had been a member of the force since 1866. He was granted £60 out of the superannuation fund and the Council found him a job as the market cleaner at twelve shillings per week.

At the end of the year the full council complemented the Chief Constable on the efficient way he had carried out his duties over the last year.

Private Constables 1880

In 1880 the council received a request from the Vicar of St Giles Church complaining about the idle and disorderly persons who were gathering in the church yard. They requested that John Whittaker and Henry Kempster be appointed constables for the purpose of keeping the church yard free of such persons. They were to come under the control of the Vicar and Church Wardens. The Watch Committee agreed. These two men must have been private constables for there is no record of them being members of the Borough force.

PC Bentley was awarded ten shillings by the Watch Committee for a "clever apprehension" of persons stealing meat from Eardley's butchers shop in Liverpool Road.

In October the Chief Constable was unfit for duty owing to illness and Sergeant Dutton was placed in charge of the force on a temporary basis.

Fire Brigade, 1880

At this time the Fire Brigade consisted of the following: the Chief Constable was captain of the brigade and the three sergeants and eleven constables were all members of the force. These were backed up by seventeen auxiliary members (part-time) with their manual pumps.

PC Dimissed for Assaulting Police! 1881

PC Cullock was ordered by the committee to send in his resignation, when it was discovered that he had been before the magistrates at Fenton charged with being drunk and disorderly and assault upon the police.

Sergeants Dutton and Deakin both had a pay increase of 7d per week, bringing their pay up to £1.11s.2d per week. At the same meeting of the Watch Committee, the chairman was given power to grant to the Chief Constable, and any other officers, leave of absence in an emergency.

It was also decided to purchase six rugs to be used for covering prisoners in the Police cells.

At the beginning of 1881, PC Wells, who had been on probation for eight weeks, was appointed to the force and George Mellor was appointed as probationary constable.

Death of Chief Constable Blyth 1881

Mr Blyth was granted further sick leave, which was extended for a further month in April. He died on 7th May, having held the office of Chief Constable for just over three years. His widow was granted £120, representing one year's pay, from the superannuation fund. On 11th March 1881, during the Chief Constable's illness, the force had been inspected again by her Majesty's Inspector, Colonel Cobb.

Chief Constable Mr Frederick Dutton 1881 - 1891

Following the death of Mr Blyth, the committee decided against advertising for a Chief Constable, filling the vacancy again from within the Borough force. They requested that applications in the candidate's own handwriting reach the committee before 2nd June. There were two applications:- Sergeant Dutton, who had been Acting Chief Constable during Mr Blyth's absence and Sergeant Deakin. Sergeant Dutton was appointed at £100 per annum, plus free house, rates, gas, coal and water.

In July, the Watch Committee decided against filling the vacant post of Sergeant but they appointed George Bagnall to the force as a probationary constable.

Two More PCs asked to Resign as Discipline Tightens

In August the Chief Constable reported to the Watch Committee that he had suspended Sergeant Swinswood and Constable Arrowsmith from duty for misconduct, as both had appeared before the Borough Magistrates charged with assault and had been fined. The Chief Constable said, *"I consider discipline and the good conduct of the Force make it imperative that I ask the committee to request that both of them resign"*. The committee agreed to the Chief Constable's request. Advertisements for two constables were then placed in the local newspapers. Numerous applications were received and six applicants were called for interview before the committee. Mr Ralph Bloor and Mr Moses Bayley were appointed constables on probation.

After interviewing six of the constables, the Watch Committee selected Eli Bentley to replace Sergeant Swinswood.

HM Inspector's Report, 1881

In October Her Majesty's Inspector was again writing to the committee complaining about the force.

> *"I observe that on 29th September you have only two Sergeants, your authorised number being three and as the force is numerically complete at 15, you have one constable in excess. It would be well for this third Sergeant to be appointed so as to regulate your duties better. You should have three in the event of a Sergeant being sick or absent, it is impossible for the remaining Sergeant to work day and night."*

The Inspector also pointed out that that as population of the Borough now stood in excess of 17,500, an increase in police strength was necessary and he hoped that the matter would be attended to after the municipal elections were over.

At the next meeting of the Watch Committee, PC Mandley was promoted to Sergeant. He had been a member of the force since 1870. PCs Bowcock and Leech were appointed to the class of Merit constable and an additional constable was appointed.

PC Rushton was fined one week's pay for being drunk on duty and his probation period was extended by two months. PC Hulme was dismissed from the force for immorality.

So ended the year - 1881 had been quite an eventful year for the Borough and its policemen!

In January 1882, the Watch Committee had 100 notices printed and put up in various places throughout the Borough. The notices stated:

Any person causing damage to property within the Borough will be dealt with to the utmost rigour of the law!

Strict Discipline Continues

PC Mellor was ordered to resign for being drunk on duty and insubordination to the Chief Constable. Mr Charles Edward Ward was his replacement.

PCs Rushton and Bloor were reported by a member of the public for drinking on duty, who alleged that they were both in the Shakespeare in George Street between 11pm and midnight on one night in March, but the charge was not substantiated. Less than ten months later PC Rushton was again before the committee, but he was not so lucky this time. He was fined two weeks pay for being drunk on duty, to be deducted at the rate of 2/6d per week. The Watch Committee were still having the police uniforms made by local tailors at this time.

Heroic Constable saves Young Boy 1883

Most forces have their heroes, and the Newcastle Police is no exception. Police Constable Bagnall was on duty in Albert Street at 6.30pm on 31st May 1883, when he received the information that a young boy named Rushton had fallen into a nearby marl pit. Hurrying to the spot, Bagnall found the boy, his head just visible above the water. Although a non-swimmer, Bagnall immediately jumped into the water and rescued the boy. Being unable to swim, Bagnall was himself in great peril and had to be helped from the pit by two men who had arrived on the scene. He was awarded a gratuity of £3 by the Watch Committee for Meritorious Conduct.

At this time the force was found yet another job, when the committee ordered that the constables were to report weekly to the manager of the gas works, all gas lamps within the Borough which were not lit at night, and the Chief Constable was to submit a monthly report to the gas committee.

During this period the Police were still issued with military-type caps.

At the beginning of 1884, a safe was purchased by the Watch Committee at a cost of £4.10s.0d. It was to be placed in the Police Office.

Juvenile Delinquency 1884

During the summer months, the Chief Constable was instructed to have one man on duty in the cemetery, from 6pm until sunset, every night. This was to stop the gangs of youths which had been gathering there and creating a nuisance. Despite this extra work the Chief Constable's request for a pay increase was refused.

Shako type helmets were issued again to replace the caps that had been in use for a number of years. For the first time the tender for uniform was given to John Hammond Ltd., who had just opened a new factory in the town. They were to supply uniforms to the Borough force for the next 62 years.

The force was still having problems with discipline, because PC Johnson was dismissed from the force for being drunk on duty. A complaint was also received by the Watch Committee alleging that PC Dobson had received money from a prostitute, but the charge was not proven.

PC Ward, who had only been in the force since 1882, had to resign due to illness. He was awarded £30 from the superannuation fund. The vacant post was filled by Mr Thomas Robert Bloor at 23/- per week. It is not known whether he was any relation to Ralph Bloor.

The whole force was paraded before the Mayor and the Watch Committee to show off the new uniforms and the Mayor told the assembly that they were *"expected to keep good order in the streets and protect the Borough."*

Good Report from Her Majesty's Inspector 1885

At the end of 1885, the force was said to be in a state of efficiency by Her Majesty's Inspector. Each officer had forty acres to cover and 1094 persons to look after. There were 68 public houses in the Borough and in the year up to the end of September the force had dealt with 143 cases of drunkenness. Nine officers had been assaulted whilst carrying out their duty.

Serious Assault on PC 1886

On April 1st 1886, PC Basford was seriously assaulted by labourer Thomas Gannon. The police had been summoned following Gannon's assault upon his own father and PC Basford went to investigate. Upon entering the house he was immediately dragged into a dark room, where four men and two women were waiting. He was thrown to the floor and everyone present began to kick and strike him all about the body. When the constable drew his staff to protect himself it was snatched from him.

His whistle was also taken away and his helmet damaged. The door had been locked to prevent his escape. When Sergeant Mandley subsequently arrived on the scene all the inmates escaped via the back door. The missing staff and whistle were never found. Gannon was sentenced to one month's imprisonment with hard labour.

Drunken PC Appears Before Court

PC Hampton's lot was not a happy one when he was found drunk and incapable by a fellow constable one warm Saturday night in Pool Dam. The Chief Constable was sent for and Hampton was whisked off to the Police Station. A doctor was summoned, who examined Hampton and pronounced him drunk. He was sent home and appeared before the local magistrates on

Monday morning, alongside all the other Saturday night drunks. He was fined ten shillings with nine shillings costs and dismissed from the force!

Good Report from HM Inspector 1887

At the end of 1887, the force boasted a total strength of sixteen, made up of one Chief Constable, three sergeants and twelve constables. Her Majesty's Inspector remarked that he was, *"...well satisfied with the force, but think the cells are totally unsuitable".*

Vandals again! Birching of Young Offenders 1888

"What are we to do with them?" asked the presiding magistrate at the Borough police court. It was Monday morning and of the eighteen defendants before him, seventeen were young boys between the ages of eight and fourteen. Seven were charged with simple larceny, two of obtaining a horse and trap by false pretences and the rest of a series of bizarre offences ranging from vagrancy to sleeping rough and stone throwing. *"I don't know what things are coming to,"* continued the magistrate, *"what these people need is a short, sharp shock. If we fine them, it will fall upon their parents, who are chiefly poor people who can ill afford to pay. I think the birch is preferably more effective."*
And so the birch was ordered in the majority of cases.

One Tuesday night in September 1888, PC Bowcock, the reserve constable had trimmed the lamps for the men going on night duty and placed them on the counter in the Police Office. He then left the room for a short time and noticed, upon his return, that three of the lamps had disappeared. A few minutes later PC Leach spotted a man passing the police office window with something bulky concealed beneath his coat. PC Leach ran outside and apprehended the man, who was found to have in his possession the three missing lamps. The following morning Robert Dillon was up before the magistrates charged with the theft from the police office on the previous night of the three lamps, valued at 10/6d. Dillon claimed that he had called at the Police Office on business but had

**Police Office
Robbed!**

been unable to find a policeman. He then said, *"I took the lamps to show them that someone had called. I had intended to take them back the following day"*. Dillon was found guilty and sentenced to one month's hard labour. He had only been released from serving his last sentence on the day prior to the offence.

**New Uniforms
1889**

It would appear, from a report in a local newspaper, that helmets of the modern type were first issued in 1889, and the report states that *"...on Saturday morning the Borough Police paraded before the Mayor and Colonel Cobb, HM Inspector of Police Forces for the Midland Counties. The men had on their new type uniforms complete with military-type helmets, which are complete with bright metal fittings"*.

**Plain clothes
Policemen used
1889**

Drunkenness seems to have been a major problem in Newcastle at this time. The Chief Constable was very concerned about the volume of drinking taking place outside the permitted hours on Sundays. All the local constables were of course known to the publicans and indeed some of them were rather too friendly with the licensees. In an attempt to control the problem, the Chief Constable of Hanley was asked to send two constables in plain clothes. These two were instructed to visit as many public houses as possible from 8am onwards on Sunday mornings. Proceedings were later taken against 15 licensees. There were at this time, 144 licensed premises in the Borough and 169 persons had been charged with drunkenness in the previous twelve months.

In November a two year old girl named Martha Jane Dodd was run over and killed by a dray belonging to Parker's Brewery of Burslem. The dray was being driven by James Jones, who was arrested for being drunk in charge of a horse and dray and later fined £2-0s-0d. with 18/6d costs.

The total cost of the force for the year 1889 was £1,421.16s.7d.

HM Inspector Complains about cells 1890

Her Majesty's Inspector Colonel Cobb had been complaining about the conditions of the Police Office for a number of years, and in particular the cells. Improvements finally came in 1890 when alterations costing £359 were carried out.

The Chief Constable, who up to this time had lived in a flat at the Police Station, was supplied with a house in Penkhull Street, for which the Council paid the rent of £25 per annum, and the Chief Constable's former flat was incorporated as part of the Police Station.

Vandalism Again! Use of Plain Clothes Policeman

The Council at this time received a large number of complaints from residents of the Borough, concerning boys and youths committing wilful damage to empty property. To combat the problem the Chief Constable decided to employ one constable on plain clothes duty, which did seem to alleviate the problem to a great extent.

According to the report of Her Majesty's Inspector, it would appear that Newcastle was paying more for its uniforms that any other force in Staffordshire. Great coats cost Wolverhampton 25/- and Newcastle 29/6d. Frock coats cost the County 21/-, Newcastle 22/9d. Trousers cost Hanley 12/3d and Newcastle 14/6d. Capes cost Hanley 16/6d and Newcastle 21/-.

Resignation of Chief Constable Mr Dutton 1891

On 1st February 1891, the Chief Constable Mr Dutton tendered his resignation due to ill health. He had been Chief Constable since 1881 and a member of the force since 1865. Although he had resigned in 1867 he had returned in 1869. Sergeant Bentley was to act as Chief Constable until a replacement was appointed.

With the Chief Constable's decision to retire, some members of the Borough council suggested again that an amalgamation with the County would be both beneficial and more economic, but when put to the vote this idea was turned down by a small majority.

**Chief Constable
Mr George Taylor
1891 - 1898**

On 19th May 1891, Sergeant and Chief Clerk at Hanley Borough Police, Mr George Taylor was appointed Chief Constable. At the time of his appointment he was 33 years of age. Born at York in 1858, Mr Taylor had trained as a teacher before joining the Halifax Borough Police in 1883, transferring to Hanley in 1885. He had been promoted to Chief Clerk in 1887.

1891 also saw the first dinner of the Borough Police and Volunteer Fire Brigade.

**New Pay rates
1892**

In April 1892 new pay rates were agreed by the Watch Committee. They gave a constable a starting rate of 22/- per week, rising to 28/- per week after ten years. Sergeants received a starting rate of 28/- per week, rising to 34/- per week after eight years of service. There was also a merit pay of 6d, 1/- and 1/6d per week. At this time each officer had one day off duty per month and seven days annual leave. The total cost of running the sixteen strong force was £1,504.12s.9d.

**First use of
Telecommunication
1893**

Communications of the modern type were used by the force on a Saturday night in June 1893. PCs Bayley and Basford were on duty in the Highland, where they found Samuel Smith drunk and acting in a violent manner.
After assaulting both constables he lay down in the road when arrested, refusing to move. One of the constables went to a nearby hotel, from where he telephoned to the Police Office, from whence the ambulance was dispatched. Smith was placed onto the ambulance, strapped down and wheeled to the Station,

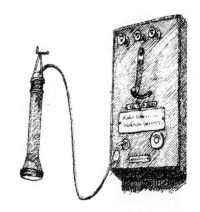

followed by a large crowd. The telephone had been installed a few months before on a trial basis.

In December 1894, a gas lamp was fixed over the entrance to the Police Office.

Inflation appears to have been around at this time because uniforms for the 16 men of the force cost £60-5s-3d as against £58-3s-8d for the previous year.

Watch Committee Sanction Spending Spree 1895

The Watch Committee were busy spending in 1895. At the beginning of the year the Chief Constable was authorised to purchase a whistle and chain for each man - until this time whistles had only been carried at night. 18 new lanterns were also purchased, the Chief Constable having informed the committee that some of their lamps had been in constant use for about thirty years. The lamps cost 4/- each. He was also asked to obtain 24 copies of the Police Constable's Guide and one copy of Snowden's Guide, at the best possible price. And in the following year, eighteen new staffs were purchased.

Sergeant Bentley Assaulted 1895

On 18th February 1895, a serious assault on Sergeant Bentley left him blind in one eye. Accompanied by Constable Bagnall, the sergeant had gone to investigate a complaint by a Mr Harvey Morris that he had been robbed of 7/- by a woman named Emma Hartshorn. The sergeant and constable went off in search of the woman and found her in the Antelope Inn, where she was arrested. She was taken out into the street, where she became extremely violent, throwing herself to the ground and refusing to get up. Sergeant Bentley was attempting to raise her from the ground when he was struck a violent blow in the face by her husband, who had just appeared on the scene. At the time that he struck Sergeant Bentley he had had the door key in his hand and it was this which caused the injury. After the attack, Samuel Hartshorne disappeared from the town. His description was circulated throughout the County and the Mayor offered a reward for Hartshorne's capture. Three days later he was arrested in Trent Vale by PC Leech of the Borough force. When charged, the prisoner said, *"I am sorry I done it. Sergeant Bentley did me no harm"*. He was later sentenced to three years penal servitude.

Firearm Incident! 1895

On a Saturday night in 1895, Josiah Simpson was charged with being drunk and disorderly and in possession of a firearm in Penkhull Street. PC Cook said that Simpson, who was a member of the Volunteers, was threatening several people with his rifle, on

35

which the bayonet was fixed. He refused to go home and was arrested before any harm could be done. He was later fined 5/-.

At the inspection of the force, Her Majesty's Inspector said that the force must be increased by at least two men, and that the cells on the ground floor should be better ventilated. This improvement was carried out at a cost of £47.8s.0d.

Sergeant Bentley Appointed first Inspector of the Borough 1895

On 16th October 1895, Sergeant Bentley was promoted to the rank of Inspector at £1.8s.0d per week. He was the first person to hold this rank within the Borough force. Sergeant Manley retired from the force at the same time, on a pension of £1.0s.5d a week. He had been a member of the force since 1870. PC Leech who was promoted to the rank of sergeant in his place.

By now the force appeared to be settling down, with one third of its members having seen over fifteen years service. The Chief Constable applied for an increase in pay and the Town Clerk was instructed to write to twenty boroughs of the same size as Newcastle to ascertain how much they paid their Chief Constables. Frederick William Clark and Charles Mace were appointed to the force.

In 1896, PC Dockery, the Detective Officer of the force, was to be allowed £5 per annum in lieu of uniform, and he was also to be issued with a macintosh coat. The £8 per year that was allowed to the Chief Constable for uniform was rescinded and he was in future to be issued with uniform.

A Day's Holiday for Queen Victoria's Diamond Jubilee 1897

To commemorate the Diamond Jubilee of Queen Victoria in 1897, each member of the force was allowed one additional day of paid holiday.

At a meeting of the Watch Committee in March 1898, the Chief Constable was told to prepare a report detailing the rates of pay of the police in boroughs with populations ranging from 16,000 to 25,000, the report to be submitted to the Watch Committee.

Chief Constable Taylor Resigns 1898

On 19th April 1898, Mr Taylor tendered his resignation, having held the post of Chief Constable for seven years. The Watch Committee instructed Inspector Bentley to act up until a replacement was appointed, for which he was to receive the same pay as the Chief Constable. Two guineas were also to be paid to Sergeant Cooke for the extra work involved in preparing the Government returns.

Chief Constable Mr John Stirling 1898 - 1901

Mr John Stirling was appointed as the Borough's eleventh Chief Constable on 4th June 1898. At the time of his appointment he held the rank of Chief Inspector with the Eastbourne Borough Police. Thirty four years of age and 6ft.3 inches tall, Mr Stirling was born in Aberdeenshire and had joined the Accrington Borough Police in 1885, transferring as a sergeant to Eastbourne upon the formation of that force in 1891. He was promoted to Inspector in 1893 and then Chief Inspector and second in command of the force twelve months later. Mr Stirling's pay as Chief Constable was £180 per year.

At the first Watch Committee meeting attended by the new Chief, he suggested to the committee that a constable clerk be appointed. The committee agreed and instructed him to advertise the post which he did in a number of newspapers. Four people were invited to an interview: Alfred Harrison of Clitheroe, Arthur Dodd from Stoke, John S Percival from Liverpool and George Ingram from Banff. Each interviewee was allowed a 3rd class return fare. George Ingram was the successful applicant, appointed at the rate of 31/6d per week.

New Pay scales 1898

On 1st October, new scales of pay came into force, replacing the rates of pay which had been in operation since 1892. Each man gained an average of an additional two shilling per week and all members of the force were issued with leggings.

Schedule of Weekly Rates of Pay 1898.

Constables

On appointment	£1.3s.11d
After 1 year	£1.5s.1d
After 2 years	£1.6s.3d

Mr George Ingram, Chief Constable 1903-12
Miss Ingram

Mr John Stirling, Chief Constable of Newcastle, 1898-1901. This photograph was taken when John Stirling was Chief Constable of Grimsby. *Grimsby Museum*

After 4 years	£1.7s.5d
After 6 years	£1.8s.7d
After 8 years	£1.9s.9d
After 10 years	£1.10s.4d

Sergeants
On appointment

After 1 year	£1.12s.8d
After 2 years	£1.13s.3d
After 4 years	£1.14s.5d
After 6 years	£1.15s.7d
After 8 years	£1.16s.9d

A Merit Class of 7d and 1/2d per week was payable to sergeants and constables on the recommendation of the Chief Constable.
With effect from 1st January 1899, the Chief Constable was instructed to pay the wages of the police in future, instead of the Borough Treasurer.

Mr Stirling was reimbursed all his expenses after passing the Weights and Measures examinations.

Inspector Bentley Retires after 30 Years 1899

April 1899 saw the retirement of Inspector Eli Bentley, who had completed thirty years of service, having held the rank of inspector since October 1895. He was granted a pension of £1.8s.0d per week, this being two thirds of his pay. Mr Bentley continued to work for the Corporation as Inspector of Weights and Measures in a civilian capacity.

In May, a telephone was installed between the Police Office and the Fire Station at a cost of £3.10s.0d per annum and in October a second telephone was installed between the Police Station and the Chief Constable's house, at a cost of £4.15s.0d per annum.

Dangerous Bicycling Reported!

The Watch Committee informed the Chief Constable that they had received numerous complaints about the furious and reckless riding of cycles in the Borough and informed him to take whatever steps he deemed necessary to put a stop to it. The Chief Constable's pay was increased to £200 per annum.

The New Century

**Chief Constable
Mr AH
Richardson
1901 - 1903**

At the beginning of 1900, the cost of clothing for the entire force was still only £81.8s.2d. It was at this time that caps were first issued to be worn with the new summer uniform. With effect from 1st June, the Chief Constable received a pay increase to £210 per annum, to be increased by £10 annually until a maximum of £250 was reached. He was also supplied with a new desk for his office.

The Watch Committee instructed the Chief Constable to purchase six pairs of India rubber gloves for the use of the police when handling broken telephone wires. The strength of the Borough force was at this time eighteen men.

In 1901, the force witnessed yet another change in leadership, when Mr Stirling left to take up the more lucrative post of Chief Constable of Grimsby Borough. He was replaced by Mr AH Richardson, who at the time of his appointment held the rank of Inspector with the Birmingham City Police. His pay was to be £180 on appointment, the same as had been paid to his predecessor upon his appointment. The Chief Clerk, PC Ingram was promoted to the rank of sergeant and his pay was increased to £1.16s.9d per week.

In December 1901, Harry Lea, a tramcar driver in the employment of the Potteries Electric Traction Co.Ltd., was charged with being drunk in charge of a tram. In court the Chief Constable said that Lea had to be forcibly removed from the tram by the police on Saturday night and placed in the cells. In mitigation Lea said that he had been treated to drink by the passengers! He was fined 10/-.

The end of year report revealed that Newcastle was the only force in Staffordshire in which every member held the St John's First Aid Certificate. The report also shows that the cost of the force was working out at the equivalent of £104.18s.10d per constable as against £80.19s.0d per constable in the County force. The other three forces in the county at that time were; Hanley, £82.12s.8d, Walsall, £87.16s.4d and Wolverhampton, £86.10s.9d.

The Chief Constable drew attention to the extra duties performed by the police in connection with the letting of the upper room of the Town Hall for concerts etc, pointing out that on each occasion the room was hired, the police had to remove the dock and witness box and place the chairs in rows, this task usually occupying three constables for up to half an hour. In addition, the police had to clean the Town Hall

windows, which occupied one man for two days. The police, claimed the Chief Constable, should be absolved from these duties. PC Davidson, who had only been a member of the force for about eighteen months, followed Mr Stirling to Grimsby to take up the appointment of Assistant Clerk.

Constable saves Child's life 1902

On 8th February 1902, PC Ralph Bloor was patrolling his beat when he was informed that a small child had just been pulled unconscious out of a bath of water into which he had fallen. Bloor hastened to the scene and commenced artificial respiration and after some fifteen minutes the two year old boy recovered. Dr Shufflebotham, upon arriving at the scene, confirmed that the constable's action had saved the child's life. Bloor was awarded £1.10s.0d by the Watch Committee.

In June the Watch Committee authorised the Chief Constable to appoint constables on probation and then bring them before the committee after six months for permanent appointment if he saw fit. Until this date, the Watch Committee had themselves interviewed all applicants.

The Chief Constable was again asking for more men and placed the following report before the Watch Committee:

"Within the last four years, the annual leave to members of the force has been increased from 7 to 10 days. During that same period their hours of duty have been reduced from 70 hours per week to 63 hours and no increase has been made to meet these reductions; of the 14 beats to be covered, only 11 constables are available. I suggest that the addition of three extra men is the absolute minimum for the efficient policing of the Borough."

The committee agreed to the appointment of one more man!

First Electric Torches, 1902

15 new helmets were purchased at 6/-each, and one cap for the Sergeant on office duty. Two electric hand torches were also purchased on a trial basis at this time. The Chief Constable, however, had to convince some members of the Watch Committee that the torches were safe to handle and were not likely to cause a shock!

Clog Fund

In December, the Borough Council decided to set up an Aid Society for clothing and boots for distribution to children in the town. They requested the cooperation of the police to inquire into deserving cases. This fund, which was to run for a number of years, became known to the people of Newcastle-under-Lyme as the Clog Fund. The year closed with the Chief Constable's report, in which he recorded that there had been 350 prosecutions for drunkenness:

Simple drunk	63
Drunk & disorderly	281
Drunk in charge of a horse	6
Total	350

Strength of Force 1903

The year 1903 opened with the state of the force as follows:

Chief Constable	1
Clerk Sergeant	1
Patrol Sergeants	3
Detective constable	1
Constables	13
Total	19

The area of the Borough was 672 acres and the population was 19,914. The average age of the force was 32 years, average height was 5 ft.10$^{1/2}$ inches and the average length of service 8$^{1/2}$ years.

One man was added to the strength of the force in this year.

Sergeant Ingram, the Chief Clerk, was promoted to the rank of inspector. He was to be paid £2.0s.0d. There had been no inspector on the force since Eli Bentley retired in April 1899.

Chief Constable George Ingram 1903 - 1912

On 15th April 1903, Mr AH Richardson tendered his resignation when he was appointed Chief Constable of Halifax Borough Police. The Watch Committee decided not to advertise the vacancy but to offer it to Inspector Ingram, who accepted the post. Sergeant Cooke was promoted to Inspector to fill Mr Ingram's post.

A letter was sent to Mr Richardson at Halifax by the Watch Committee, thanking him for his services to the Borough, which he had always carried out in a most efficient way.

Helmets for night duty, with black metal fittings, were issued for the first time.

The Watch Committee agreed to the Chief Constable's suggestion to have telephone call bells installed in the houses of the firemen, since the ringing of the fire bell, which was situated at the top of the Police Office, caused large crowds to gather which created a nuisance outside the office!

The Motor Car Arrives 1904

The Chief Constable's report for 1904 mentions a motor car for the first time. In his report he states that one person was charged under the Motor Car Act, one person was charged with being drunk in charge of a horse and one reported for riding a bicycle without lights. The Watch Committee asked the council to place a notice board at the top of Hassell Street, warning motorists of the dangerous incline.

Runaway horses seem to have been causing problems to the people of Newcastle and its policemen at this time. PC John

**Runaway Horses
1904**

Morgan was on duty at 3.30pm one Monday in March 1904, when a horse pulling a bread van suddenly bolted along the road at a furious rate. At considerable risk to himself PC Morgan managed to bring the horse to a stop. He was awarded 10/6d for Meritorious Conduct.

In July of the same year PC Delancey was on duty in Red Lion Square when a pony attached to a Mailcart was frightened by an electric tramcar and bolted along the High Street. throwing the driver to the ground. The constable managed to bring the pony to a halt just before it was about to dash into a shop window. PC Delancey was also awarded 10/6d.

The following year PC Eaton was on duty in the High Street when a horse standing in the street became restive and bolted along the road. PC Eaton caught hold of the reins and, whilst attempting to stop the horse, his cape became caught up in the shaft of the cart. He was dragged along the road and the wheels of the cart passed over him. Injuries to his back and abdomen necessitated his removal to hospital and he was off sick for a total of 36 days! He had only been back for a few days when, remarkably, again on duty in the High Street, a pony attached to a trap bolted, throwing the occupant to the ground. The constable managed to stop the pony and rendered first aid to the occupant!(One wonders if he suffered from 'post traumatic stress'?)

PC Bowcock, who had been a member of the force since 1876, retired on a weekly pension of £1.1s.0d, this being two thirds of his weekly pay.

Mr Ingram, the Chief Constable moved from his home in Vessey Terrace to one in Seabridge Road, the telephone also moving with him.

**Cooperation
Between Forces
1905**

In 1905 it was decided to issue the men with straw helmets for summer use. They were obtained from J Anderson & Co, Luton, at a cost of 7/- each.

The Chief Constable reported to the Watch Committee that

Inspector Cook, Sergeant Bloor, PCs Connolly and Rawlinson had each been awarded 10/- by the Chief Constable of Staffordshire for their help in tracing and apprehending a number of persons wanted by the County force for indictable offences.

PC Assaulted 1905

At 1.25am on Thursday 11th November 1905, PC Knight was on duty in Penkhull Street when he saw a man acting suspiciously. As he approached him the man ran away into Paradise Street. PC Knight gave chase and found him in an empty shed. Catching hold of the man he began to drag him into the street when he was suddenly dealt a violent blow on the head. Realising that he had more than one person to deal with he drew his staff, but before he had a chance to use it, it was snatched from him and he was struck about the head and face. He was also kicked several times whilst lying on the ground. Both assailants made good their escape. The parcels that they carried, containing beef, pork and boots were found later and identified as the proceeds of a robbery at Stoke.

The Chief Constable had his pay increased to £200 per annum.

Gift Horse!

On 10th November 1905 a grey gelding was found straying in Stafford Street and impounded by the police. Although advertised in the local newspaper, the gelding remained unclaimed. On 23rd November, still unclaimed, the horse was sold at public auction and after all the costs had been met the Chief Constable had a balance of 9/4d which was paid into the general rates.

First Police Surgeon 1905

The Watch Committee decided that in future no deductions were to be made from the men's pay when they were off duty due to sickness. At the end of the year, Dr Morris was appointed Police Surgeon at £20 per annum. The following tender for uniformwas submitted in 1906:

Chief Constable;	1 patrol jacket,
	2 prs. trousers,
	2 prs, brown leather gloves,
	1 cap.
Inspector;	as above.
Sergeants;	3 tunics, 3 serge jackets.
Clerk Sergeant;	1 office jacket, 1 cap.

Constables;	14 tunics,
	14 serge jackets,
	18 prs. serge trousers,
	18 prs. dress trousers,
	18 prs. black worsted gloves,
	36 prs. white cotton gloves.
	Total costs; £68
	Suppliers; John Hammond & Co.

Mutual Aid 1906

The Chief Constable reported to the Watch Committee that he would require twenty extra constables for duty at the General Election, to be held in February 1900. He was told to make the necessary arrangements, and he later informed the Watch Committee that the Chief Constable of Staffordshire had placed at his disposal thirty men, free of charge. At the suggestion of the Chief Constable the Watch Committee allowed all the Borough men one day's additional pay. A letter was also sent by the committee to Captain, the Honourable G A Anson, Chief Constable of Staffrdshire, thanking him for the services of his men.

Two years later the following communication was received from the Chief Constable of the County:

Agreement under Police Act, 1890

Sir

I hereby ask you to cancel any standing agreement which I may have made with you at any time for the loan of constables under the Police Act of 1890. I do not wish to enter into any standing agreement for the loan of men, as even under such agreement the actual loan of men necessarily involves fresh arrangements which amount to much the same thing as a fresh agreement. In the case of an emergency I would, as here-to-after, very gladly do my best to comply with any request for assistance, but in my opinion it is preferable when such assistance is required to make such agreement merely for the particular occasion.

G A Anson
C C Staffordshire
25th May 1908

Police Convalescent Home

Sergeant Johnson was the first member of the Newcastle force to be sent to the Police Convalescent Home at Harrogate. He had been away from duty on sick leave for 56 days and the Police

Surgeon thought that fourteen days at the home would be of benefit to him.

Home Office Detectives Offered 1906

A letter was received from the Home Office in May 1906, offering the services of detectives of special skill and experience to help in exceptionally difficult investigations. A copy of this letter was sent to every Chief Constable in the country.

HM Inspector's Report 1906

His Majesty's Inspector inspected the force in September and made the following recommendations:
1. That a woman be employed to look after the female prisoners.
2. Electric call bells be fitted to each cell.
These recommendations were put into effect two months later.

The following members of the force were disciplined in 1906:
PC Chattin - fined 2/6d for Neglect of Duty - failing to attend court as a witness.
PC Price - also fined 2/6d for the same offence.
PC Delancey - fined 2/6d for Neglect of Duty. - failing to work his beat properly.
PC Haywood - stopped one day's leave for being 25 minutes late for duty.
PC Dyke - stopped one day's leave for Neglect of Duty. - failing to dust and prepare the Town Hall for Police Court.

Sergeant Bayley retired from the force in November, having completed 25 years service. He was awarded an annual pension of £54.2s.0d.

The following constables were interviewed by the Watch Committee for the post of sergeant: PCs Connolly, Cotton, Morgan, Knight, Welch, Eaton, Scott and Price.
PC Connolly was promoted.

In January 1907, the Chief Constable requested permission to purchase from Enderley Mills a suit of plain clothes for the force detective. This was granted provided that the price did not exceed the cost of a uniform.

PC Byatt Thompson was appointed to the force and later in the year, three more men were appointed to fill vacancies: Joseph Davis, James Morris, William Short.

Strong Discipline Continues 1907

Both Sergeant Johnson and PC Morgan appeared before the Watch Committee in February to answer charges against them. Sergeant Johnson was asked to resign and PC Morgan demoted to 4th Class. In the March.
PC Eaton left the force, transferring to Durham County - only to return four years later.

On 17th December, PC Heywood, who had been a force member since 1902, and had been away from duty due to sickness for five months, was pensioned out of the force. He had been in the North Staffordshire Infirmary for a total of 133 days and the surgeon stated that he would not recover. He was taken to his parents' home, Baschurch near to Oswestry in Shropshire, a distance of about forty miles, by horsedrawn ambulance - it is not recorded how long the journey took! He died on the 3rd January 1908. Sergeant Bloor and PCs Gilles, Davis and Price attended the funeral and later submitted a request to the Watch Committee that their expenses be refunded.

HM Inspector's Report 1908

His Majesty's Inspector Lieut. Col. Eden inspected the force in April 1908 and again brought to the attention of the Watch Committee the need to appoint a female to attend to the women prisoners. The H M I also recommended that the cells on the ground floor be fitted with a W C.

An application from the inspector, sergeants and constables that the Police Christmas Fund be revived was refused by the committee.
The Chief Constable's pay was increased to £220 per annum.
The sergeants and constables also placed before the Watch Committee an application for a pay increase, but they had to wait almost twelve months for it to be approved. The increase was not particularly generous, considering that it was replacing pay scales which had been in operation since 1898. It awarded each man an average 1/- per week and the Inspector £5 per year.

In January 1909, the Chief Constable was instructed by the Watch Committee to inform the members of the force that deductions from pay for the superannuation fund would not, in future, be refunded, except in exceptional circumstances.

Seventeen day and seventeen night duty belts were purchased, also sixteen new lamps and seventeen pairs of new leggings - the Chief Constable said that the present ones were ten years old.

Sergeant Bloor retired from the force on a pension of £63.14s.0d per annum. He had over 28 years service. PC Cotton was promoted to fill the vacancy.

Good Report from HM Inspector 1909 Mounted Police Proposed

His Majesty's Inspector visited and inspected the force in June, afterwards stating that he was *"very pleased with what I have seen, the men parade and drill very well. The alterations to the cells have been carried out and a female has been engaged to look after the women prisoners"*. The HMI suggested to the Watch Committee that they should consider having a number of officers mounted, so as to be available in the case of emergency, adding that this was a recommendation from the Home Office. Arrangements were made locally to hire horses as and when the Chief Constable thought fit.

The Chief Constable suggested to the Watch Committee that in future dogs found by the police should be kept in the cellar of the Police Station, instead of the Town Yard in Goose Street. The cellar was white washed and used to house the dogs - but not for long. The Council was soon receiving complaints from people living nearby, that they were being kept awake at night by barking dogs. The Chief Constable requested that the committee provide more suitable premises!

Three new members appointed in May were not to remain long with the force; PC Cope resigned in March of the following year and PCs Price and Johnson were to quit after only five months of service. Sergeants Cotton and Connolly submitted a report on PC Price to the Watch Committee and his resignation was requested. PC Johnson was ordered to resign forthwith for insubordination to the sergeant. The discipline problems of forty years ago seemed to be repeating themselves!

Miners' Strike and Serious Disturbances 1909

The night of Thursday 8th July 1909 was destined to be a night to be remembered by the people of Newcastle. North Staffordshire had been in the grip of a miner's strike since the previous Tuesday. On Thursday afternoon four colliers had been arrested at Silverdale by the County Police and charged with riotous conduct before being taken to Newcastle and lodged in the Borough Police Station (the County police station in Water Street was not opened until 1912). This fact soon became known and in the course of the evening a crowd of several thousand, mostly colliers, congregated outside the Police Station. The attitude of some of the men became serious.

The Chief Constable Mr Ingram had received information that a large number of colliers from Tunstall, Silverdale and Chesterton were making their way towards the town and he had requested assistance from the County Police, who drafted seventy men into Newcastle, some of whom were mounted. Quite a number of these County men were conveyed by tramcar into the Borough, from the surrounding Pottery towns.

The strength of the police was now such that they were able to prevent any assault with the intent of releasing the prisoners from custody. Realising that any attack upon the Police Station was now out of the question, the mob commenced to throw stones and other missiles at the Police.

The order was given for the force to draw their batons and charge, driving the crowd back along High Street. Little damage was done, for the crowd managed to dodge the batons. There were several more charges into the crowd, during which two of the Borough policemen, Sergeant Connolly and PC Chatwin were struck with stones hurled by the mob. Chatwin was hit on the back of the neck and needed medical attention.

The County authorities decided to free the four prisoners on bail and this was done by releasing the men one at a time. This seemed to have a calming effect upon the crowd and at around 10.30pm they began to drift away, but it was two more hours before all the streets were quiet again.

Cinematograph Act 1910

In 1910 the Chief Constable became the Inspector under the Cinematograph Act, which came into being on 1st January that year.

Police Weekly Rest Day Act 1910

The Chief Constable addressed the Watch Committee concerning the Police Weekly Rest Day Act, which was before Parliament and due to come into effect four years later. The Chief Constable pointed out that the leave taken by the force would increase from 247 to 988 days per annum. Nothing appears to have been done in regard to the implementation of the Act and in November 1911 members of the Borough force petitioned the Watch Committee, asking them to adopt the Police Weekly Rest Day Act without delay. After talks with the Chief Constable, the committee agreed that from February 1912 each man would have one day off in fourteen and that the Act would be adopted in full from 1st April 1913. To compensate, the force was increased by two men. The precious rest days, however, were not to last, as they were curtailed by the outbreak of the First World War in 1914. It was to be 1919 before they were fully re-instated again.

In June the Watch Committee stated that in future no member of the force would receive a pay increase without first making an application to the committee via the Chief Constable.

Praise for Force in Quote From Chief Constable's Annual Report 1910

The Recorder of Newcastle, Mr A Jones-David, made the following statement before the quarter sessions in March:

"I have read the annual report of the Chief Constable of the Borough and find it a very interesting document. I wonder how many people of Newcastle know that the average age of the policemen in the Borough is between 32 and 33 years and the average height is 5ft. 11$^{1/2}$ inches. They have what I think of as a comparatively small staff, but they have in that staff a set of men absolutely in the prime of life. I dare say that it is due to the efficient discharge of their duties that there is so little crime to deal with, in a well governed town. The true criteria of the efficiency of the police is not the number of cases before the courts and the number of convictions achieved. The true efficiency of good police management is the prevention and not the punishment of crime and in that respect Newcastle stands very well."

In 1911, after an eighteen month wait, the Chief Constable finally

received a response to the problem of the barking dogs, when it was decided that a shelter for stray dogs would be built at the town destructors. The Sanitary Committee would then take charge of all stray and unwanted dogs at a cost of 3d per dog per day and 1/- for each dog that they put down by poisoning.

Traffic Survey 1911

In February 1911, a traffic survey showed the following totals had passed through a point in one week:

Bicycles	*1,316*
Motor cars	*299*
Motor Cycles	*28*
Two wheeled horse carts	*2,115*
Four wheeled horse carts	*628*

PC Bate Appointed and Tight Discipline Continues 1911

Wesley Bate of Cosford, Shropshire, was appointed constable in the force on 8th May 1911.

In the same month, PC de Lancey was before the committee to answer the following charges:

1. That he failed to produce his appointments when requested to do so on parade.

2. That he failed to give a satisfactory explanation of their whereabouts.

De Lancey was demoted and fined 1/2d per week for the next year. Two weeks later he was again up before the committee on two further charges;

1. Failing to work his beat properly.

2. Being found to be under the influence of drink when on duty.

At this point, he was dismissed from the force forthwith.

Inspector Cook and Sergeant Connolly each received the George V Coronation Medal.

An extract from the Chief Constable's report for the month of January, 1911 reads as follows:

Since your last meeting 5 crimes have been reported to the police and in connection therewith 4 persons have been arrested and dealt with summarily. Property to the value of £1-6s-10d has been reported stolen, of which £1.1s.0d has been recovered. Proceedings have also been taken against 37 males and 20 females for the following offences:

CRIME	*PROCEEDINGS*	*CONVICTIONS*
Assault common	*2*	*2*
Chimney on fire	*3*	*3*
Crying Watercress!'		
on the Lord's Day:	*1*	*0*
Drunkenness:	*3*	*3*
Drunk on licensed premises:	*2*	*2*
Deserting from Army:	*1*	*1 to await escort*
Falsely representing to be		
a deserter from Army:	*1*	*0*
Indecent behaviour:	*2*	*2*
Keeping a dog without a licence: 1		*1*
Misbehaviour as a pauper:	*2*	*2*
Obscene language:	*3*	*2*
Prevention of Crimes Act:	*1*	*1*
Riding a bicycle without lights: 1		*1*
Riotous behaviour:	*33*	*26*
Married Woman's Act:	*1 application*	*0 order made*

Crying "Watercress" on the Lord's day!

The year of 1912 started with a slight alteration to the men's uniform. The chief clerk was to have a single chevron with a crown above and the Merit Class constable was to have a single chevron on the right arm.

At the Watch Committee meeting of February 1912 the Chief Constable suggested that one of the constables be made acting sergeant, but the committee decided against this and promoted PC Giles, the clerk constable to sergeant with effect from 1st April. His pay was to be £1.14s.5d per week. It was also decided that Inspector Cook was to take his turn of night duty. PC Price was reported to the Watch Committee for being drunk on duty. He was fined 10/- and received a severe reprimand.

County Police Presence Because of National Miners' Strike 1912

Between February and April 1912 a large contingent of County police were stationed in the town, because of the Miners' Strike. There were no coal mines situated within the precincts of the Borough at that time, but the town was a focal point for a number of mines and mining villages. It was also the headquarters

of a division of the County Police. Doubtless the authorities were taking precautions against a repetition of the troubles of three years earlier, but there were no serious disturbances reported within the Borough during the strike.

Resignation of Chief Constable Ingram

In June 1912, the Chief Constable Mr G Ingram tendered his resignation to the committee due to ill health. He had been the Chief Constable since 1903.

At the meeting of the Watch Committee some members were again in favour of amalgamation with the County and suggested that the Town Clerk communicate with the County Police Authority to find out the terms under which the County would be willing to police the Borough. The resolution was lost on a vote of 5 to 3. The Town Clerk was instructed to advertise for a replacement to the Chief Constable and on 19th July 1912 the Watch Committee met to select the Borough's 14th Chief Constable. The following eight candidates were called for interview:

Inspector P Ingram	Southport
Inspector W Forster	Grimsby
Inspector T Danby	Peterborough
Inspector T Lee	Chesterfield
Inspector F Davies	Stoke-on-Trent
Inspector P Berry	Stoke-on-Trent
Inspector W Cox	Cambridge
Sergeant C V Gilles	Newcastle

Chief Constable Wiliam Forster 1912 - 1932

After careful consideration, the Watch Committee chose Inspector William Forster of Grimsby and he took up his duties on the 12th August. At the time of his appointment he was 41 years of age and had a total of 18 years police service. He was born in Cumberland and joined the Wigan Borough Police in 1894, transferring to Leeds a few years later as a shorthand clerk. In 1900 he went to Grimsby as Chief Clerk and was promoted to Inspector in 1910. One wonders if a testimonial from the Chief Constable of Grimsby, Mr J Stirling, himself a former Chief Constable of Newcastle, had any bearing on Mr Forster's appointment. His pay was to be £180 per annum, rising by annual increments of £5 to a maximum of £250.

The new Chief Constable had not long been in office when another job was thrust upon him. He was appointed Inspector of Hackney Carriages and then, in the November, the Chief Constable, along with PCs Rawlins and Philips were made Inspectors under the Shops Act.

Mr Forster brought with him from Grimsby a system whereby the owners of property and shops in the town were able to leave their keys at the police station upon payment of 10/6d per year. The police were able to gain access to the property in case of fire, etc. This system was to create problems for the force in later years.

Mick the Mascot 1912

In 1912 the force became the unofficial owners of a dog. The local newspaper report reads:

> *"For the last two years a sturdy Irish terrier has been seen accompanying various members of the Borough Police Force on their beats, often at night as well as during the day, and visitors to the Police Station have grown accustomed to seeing Mick stretched out in luxurious ease before the charge room fire. Mick's liking for policemen can be traced back to barrack life in the army, for he is the property of Captain Gifford, Adjutant of the 5th North Staffordshire Regiment. Captain Gifford is to leave Newcastle and return to his regiment in India and he has decided to leave Mick to live with his policeman friends, and so has presented him as a gift to the force."*

The Staffordshire Agricultural Show was held in the town in June and seven constables were brought out to perform traffic duty in their own time. The Chief Constable made an application to the Watch Committee that they be paid for this extra duty and the committee agreed.

The year ended with the Chief Constable holding the following appointments:

Inspector under the Cinematograph Act
Inspector under the Shops Act

Inspector of Common Lodging Houses
Inspector under the Disease of Animals Act
Inspector under the Petroleum Act

With Mr Forster's pay standing at £180 per year, the Council were getting good value for their money!

At the beginning of 1913, when Mr Forster had only been five months in office, he placed the following report before the Watch Committee:

> *"There is no apparatus at the police office for testing the petroleum and without one I am unable to say if a licence is required or not. Secondly I ask the committee to purchase a card index system for registering and recording prisoner's convictions. And finally, there is no typewriter at the police office and I intend to ask the committee to purchase one."*

The Chief Constable was instructed to purchase a card index system and petroleum tester without delay and was informed that a typewriter would be bought out of the following year's estimates. No doubt the Chief Constable returned to his office a happier man.

Mr Forster's next action was to negotiate better pay for his men. At the February meeting of the Watch Committee he said that in the last two years nearly every police force in England had had an increase in pay. The men of the Newcastle Borough Force had not received any such increase, nor had they made any such application. *"I think in all fairness to them, it should be considered. I have placed before this committee, a list of pay applicable to adjoining forces and from it you will see that our men are a good way behind."*

On 1st April 1913 the following pay scale was adopted, replacing the pay scale which had been in use since 1908.

Inspectors:	Old Rate	New Rate p.a.
On appointment:	£98.16. 0d	£106.12s.0d
After 3 years	£104.0s.0d	£109.4s.0d
After 6 years	£109.0s.0d	£111.16s.0d
After 9 years	£114.0s.0d	£117.0s.0d
After 12 years	£119.0s.0d	£122.4s.0d

Sergeants		per week
On appointment	£1.14s.5d	£1.15s.0d
After 1 year	£1.15s.0d	£1.15s.7d
After 2 years	£1.15s.7d	£1.16s.2d
After 4 years	£1.16s.2d	£1.16s.9d
After 8 years	£1.17s.11d	£1.17s.11d
After 10 years	£1.18s.6d	£1.19s.1d
Second Class Merit	£1.19s.1d	
First Class Merit	£1.19s. 8d	
Constables		
On appointment	t£1.5s.1d	£1.6s.3d
After 1 year	£1.6s.3d	£1.6s.10d
After 2 years	£1.7s.5d	£1.9s.2d
After 4 years	£1.8s.7d	£1.16s.9d
After 6 years	£1.9s.2d	£1.9s.9d
After 8 years	£1.9s.9d	£1.10s.4d
After 10 years	£1.10s.4d	£1.10s.11d
After 12 years	£1.11s.6d	£1.12s.1d
Second Class Merit	£1.12s.1d	
First Class Merit	£1.12s.8d	

There was also a Merit Class payment to sergeants and constables of one halfpenny per week.

Royal Visit to Borough 1913

King George V paid a Royal visit to the Borough in April 1913. Large crowds were expected and to help control them 53 officers, three of whom were mounted, were loaned by the County. The County Authority later submitted a bill for £18.3s.10d.

The Chief Constable reported to the committee that in future convicted prisoners would not be marched through the streets in handcuffs to the railway station. He had been instructed henceforth to hire a conveyance and charge it to the prison commissioners.

Strike at Enderley Mills 1913

In September, a strike took place at Enderley Mills and lasted for three weeks. Nearly one thousand workers, mainly women and girls, were idle. On Monday of the second week the management announced that the mill would be open to those operatives who

Newcastle under Lyme Borough Police 1913

John Norcup

left to right:
Back Row; PCs Robinson, Beeston, Ford. **Mounted:** PC Rawlinson, Sgt. Gillies.
Middle Row; PCs Phillips, Bate, Eaton, Watkins, Black, Plant, Byatt, Hawley, Lowe, Detective Morris.
Front Row; PCs Knight, Welch, Sgt. Cotton, C.C. Forster, Mr WM Mellard, Mayor, Insp. Cook, Sgt. Connolly, PC's Morgan, Chattin.

and Police Dog Mick

desired to return to work. About eighty girls presented themselves at the mill on Tuesday morning, just before 7.00am. A large body of strikers awaited them at the gates and, despite the large number of police officers present, many of the girls were roughly handled and some actually assaulted. The scene was repeated when the girls returned to the mill after dinner. When the workers left the mill in the evening, a large crowd was gathered in Enderley Street and disorderly scenes ensued. The police decided that the girls should be escorted to their homes in small groups, but they were followed by the strikers, who threw stones and other missiles at both the workers and the police. Eight women later appeared before the Borough Police Court on various charges, including assault on the Chief Constable. During the strike the Chief Constable was unable to maintain order with the small force available to him and it became necessary to borrow 25 men from the Stoke-on-Trent Force.

At the end of the year, Clerk Sergeant Gilles left the force, having received a promotion to Inspector with the Shrewsbury Borough Force. He had applied for the post of Chief Constable when it had become available in 1912, but that post had, of course, gone to Mr Forster.

In March 1914, thirteen members of the force sat the First Aid Ambulance examination and all passed. A deputation of constables called on the Watch Committee in June, requesting an improvement in pay and conditions of service, namely eight hour shifts and more annual leave. The committee agreed to look at the men's complaint.

The First World War 1914

Britain entered into the Great War in August 1914. The impact was felt by the entire population and the people of the Borough and its policemen were no exception. PCs Ford and Robinson, who were army reservists, were immediately called back to join their regiments, and PC Eaton, along with the detective officer PC Morris, went to Lichfield Barracks as drill instructors on loan to the army. Before the month was out the force was to lose another member when PC Pointon enlisted. Due to the depletion of the force, the Chief Constable had to suspend all rota

and annual leave. He did, however, allow two men off duty during the day on Sundays.

The Chief Constable reported to the Watch Committee that at the end of August he had received notification from the Home Office with details concerning the formation of a first Police Reserve in the Borough. The reserve was not to exceed 25 men, comprising three sergeants and twenty-two constables. They would receive 7/6d per annum for sergeants and 5/- per annum for constables, plus 7/6d and 5/- per annum respectively if they put in at least three drills during the year. The men were to be prepared to parade for duty immediately when called upon and would receive 7/6d and 5/- respectively per day when on duty.

The Watch Committee decided to take no further action on this matter, but instructed the Chief Constable to try and fill the three vacancies caused by the men who have joined the army.

At the same meeting the Chief Constable was told to take whatever action he deemed necessary with regard to enemy aliens within the Borough. The committee undertook to indemnify him against all consequences of such action!

Licensees of public houses in the town said that they would refuse to serve women before 11am in the morning and that men in the King's Uniform would not be served after 10pm at night, to take effect from the 1st December.

The Chief Constable was instructed to obtain tenders from within the Borough for the following year for uniform. The total cost for the uniform, including leggings and helmets for the entire force was £114.11s.8d.

In November the Watch Committee said that they were unable to fix a new pay scale for the members of the force and that it would be deferred until a new pay scale was adopted by the County Police.

**PC Welch killed
by a Tram
1915**

The new year was only a few days old when the force lost one of its longest serving officers. At about seven o'clock on the evening of 8th January 1915, PC John Welch was crossing the Ironmarket from the direction of the Municipal Hall (where the library now stands) to the Post Office, when he was knocked down by the Newcastle to Stoke tram. The constable was carried into the post office and a doctor sent for. After a quick examination, he was taken to the North Staffordshire Infirmary, where he died some five hours later from a fractured skull.

PC Welch had been a member of the force since 1898. He left a widow and a nineteen year old daughter. His widow received a small pension of £15 per annum and the Potteries Electric Traction Co. Ltd. sent her a cheque for £25. The Member of Parliament for Newcastle, Mr JC Wedgwood had an interview with the Home Secretary to try and obtain a better pension for the widow but was told that it was not possible to grant a pension higher than the one provided by statute.

Four men were appointed to the force in February, to fill existing vacancies.

The Chief Constable received a pay increase, with effect from the 1st April to £235 and then on the 12th August to £245 and then by £10 increments per annum until a maximum of £275. At the same meeting a new pay scale was announced for constables and

New Pay Scales 1915

sergeants, also effective from 1st April.

Sergeants

On appointment	£1.19s.0d per week
After 2 years service	£2.0s.0d per week
After 4 years service	£2.1s.0d per week
After 6 years service	£2.2s.0d per week
After 8 years service	£2.3s.0d per week
After 10 years service	£2.4s.0d per week

Constables

On appointment	£1.8s.0d per week
After 12 months service	£1.9s.0d per week
After 2 years service	£1.10s.0d per week
After 4 years service	£1.11s.0d per week
After 6 years service	£1.12s.0d per week
After 8 years service	£1.13s.0d per week
After 10 years service	£1.14s.0d per week
After 12 years service	£1.15s.0d per week
After 16 years service	£1.16s.0d per week
Merit Class	1/6d per week extra.

Pubs Close Early 1915

Major Savill, the Commanding Officer of the 3rd Reserve Infantry Brigade, made an order under the Defence of the Realm Act, closing all licensed premises in Newcastle at 9pm.

Assaults on PCs 1915

The Chief Constable reported to the Watch Committee in April that he was concerned about the increasing number of assaults on police constables in the town. There had been 11 such cases during the preceding year and the Chief Constable appealed to those members of the committee who were magistrates to consider carefully before passing lenient sentences for such offences.

Inspector Cook retired from the force in October, having completed 28 years service. PC Rawlinson was promoted to sergeant on the same date, but the vacancy of inspector was not filled. Inspector Cook received a pension of £1.14s.0d per week.

In September the Chief Constable made the following statement to the Watch Committee:

"I wish to draw the committee's attention to the increasing rowdiness that is taking place in Baker Street. As you know, this street is a cul-de-sac and at the present time houses a population of about 95, not including some 25 who have enlisted. During the last five months proceedings have been taken in 13 cases against residents for riotous behaviour, abusive language, wilful damage, etc., but this is only a small fraction of the offences which have actually occurred. If any means could be devised so that there would be an outlet at each end of the street, we could supervise it much more effectively. The continual uproars there are a nuisance to the neighbourhood. Baker Street is in a notorious part of the town where the police usually patrol in twos."

Drinking on duty was to be the downfall of yet another member of the Borough force. At 9.15pm on the 7th December 1915, PC Plant was found drunk on duty by the sergeant and escorted to the Police Station. The Chief Constable was called from his home to the station, where he saw Plant. He then decided that the constable was in such a state that it was not safe to send him home by himself and ordered Sergeant Rawlinson to accompany him. The following day, Plant was ordered to resign. He had been a member of the force since 1909.

Three more members of the force joined the colours in November, followed by two more in January.

1916

The year 1916 opened with the force much reduced in manpower, but with the help of the Special Constabulary, law and order was still maintained in the Borough. The Chief Constable reported a decrease in the amount of crime committed in the town at this time, which was no doubt due to the number of men who were away fighting for King and Country.

PC Morris, the detective officer who had been acting as a drill instructor with the Army since the outbreak of war in 1914, returned to the police force in April. The Chief Constable was able to employ him on uniform street duty, because there was insufficient crime to keep a detective officer fully employed.

First Boy Clerk 1916

In March, the force lost another officer to the Army when PC Wesley Bate, who had been acting as clerk, was called up for military service. The vacancy left by Bate was filled when 16 year old Leonard Hobson was appointed the forces first civilian boy clerk at 15/- per week.

The constable and sergeants made an application to the Watch Committee in May for a War bonus to be paid to them. The Chief Constable was instructed to inquire from other forces about this and to find out what they paid to their men. On 1st October it was agreed that married men would get 4/- and single men 3/- per week. Twelve months later this was to be increased to put them in the following scale, the same as that paid to the county men.

Constables	**9/-per week**
Sergeants	**8/-per week plus 1/- per child**

An increase was also paid to the wives and children of men serving in HM Forces. There was also a 5d per week increase in the Boot Allowance paid to each officer.

On the final day of June, Mr Eli Bentley retired from the post of Weights and Measures Inspector. He had held the post for 17 years. The Watch Committee decided not to appoint another Inspector at that time, but the Chief Constable was to act as adjuster under the act and also prosecute all infringements at court. He was awarded a pay increase of £40 per annum for the extra work involved.

Special Constables Paraded for HM Inspector 1916

In June 1916, Colonel Tomasson, His Majesty's Inspector, visited the Borough force. There were 60 Special Constables on the parade. It was at this time that ambulance classes were arranged for all Specials wishing to attend.

The year 1917 seems to have been very quiet as far as the Newcastle Borough police force was concerned. Boy clerk, L Hobson had his pay increased to £1 per week and an additional boy clerk, Alfred Rawlinson, was employed at 15/- per week.

More men leave Force to join Army 1917

In April 1917, Constable Samuel Lowe, who had enlisted in the army in August 1915, received a commission. Both the Chief Constable and the Watch Committee sent him a letter of congratulation. Two more members, PCs Phillips and Hawley, joined the army the following month. Out of the authorised strength of 23 men, 15 served in the Great War between 1914-1918.

Special Constables were now being used on an increasing scale to help with the policing of the town. There duties were now to patrol the town from 6am to 6pm on week days, each man working a 4 hour shift. On the first Sunday of each month, the Specials policed the town alone from 6am to 10pm. Two special constables received a commendation from the Watch Committee in the September, when they apprehended a youth who was breaking into a gas meter, which helped to clear up a number of similar crimes that had taken place in that area of town

In March 1918, the Watch Committee agreed to make a donation of £2.2s.0d per year to the police orphanage in Harrogate. At the same meeting the Watch Committee increased the War bonus to 15/- per week. Police officers who were serving with HM Forces were still promoted to the years's service class when it became due.

The members of the force placed an application before the Watch Committee in July, requesting an increase in pay. They were told that this would be deferred until they had heard what the County had offered their men. They did not have long to wait because on the 1st September 1918, the following rate was adopted:

Constables

On appointment	£2.3s.0d per week
After 1 years service	£2.4s.0d per week
After 2 years service	£2.5s.0d per week
After 3 years service	£2.6s.0d per week
After 4 years service	£2.7s.0d per week
After 5 years service	£2.8s.0d per week
After 6 years service	£2.9s.0d per week
After 7 years service	£2.10s.0d per week
After 8 years service	£2.11s.0d per week
After 15 years service	£2.12s.0d per week
After 20 years service	£2.13s.0d Maximum
Merit Class	1/6d per week extra.

Sergeants

On appointment	£2.16s.0d per week
After 2 years service	£2.17s.0d per week
After 4 years service	£2.18s.0d per week
After 6 years service	£2.19s.0d per week
After 8 years service	£3.0s.0d per week

All ranks 10/- per week extra after 26 years service.
All ranks 10/- per week war bonus plus 2/6d for each child under 14 years of age.
In future all pay and conditions will be the same as those applying to the County Police.

End of Great War 1918

At the end of the year, PCs Dutton and Hawley returned to the force after service in the army.

Return from Military service 1919

The new year started well for the force - the year was only a few days old when two more former members rejoined after service with HM Forces. PC Ford returned in February but, owing

to a back injury sustained in the war and a report from the police doctor, the Watch Committee were unable to offer him his old job back. The committee did, however, offer Ford the post of Inspector of Weights and Measures for the Borough, if he could pass the Board of Trade Examination, for which the Council offered to pay.

The Chief Constable was now being paid £354 per annum.

Detention House for Children

With effect from 1st April 1919, the home of PC Beeston at 51 Stibbs Gate was utilised as a house of detention for children and he and his wife were allowed £15 per annum for this use.

In May 1919 members of the force sent a petition to the Watch Committee, asking for a reduction in working hours and for the adoption of the eight hour day. They also requested an extension of annual leave. In reply, the committee agreed to the eight hour day as soon as the Chief Constable was able to arrange matters, but the extra leave was to be deferred until all members had returned from the HM Forces.

Threatened Police Strike 1919

The Watch Committee must have heard rumours about the pending police strike because in June they issued the following notice to all members:

"Any police officer of any rank in the Newcastle Borough Police who fails to report in the ordinary course of duty, or when called upon, will be forthwith dismissed from the force and will not be permitted to rejoin. Dismissal will result in the loss of all service counting towards pension."

Along with all other forces in the County, Newcastle adopted the National Pay Scale in September 1919. Before the year ended, three more members of the force returned from war service. The Chief Constable's report for 1919 contained the following information:

Authorised strength of the force	**23 men**
Served in the Great War	**15 men (60%)**
Killed in Action	**2 men**
Returned to duty this date	**6 men**
Invalided	**1 man**

Still serving in army	**6 men**
Commissioned	**1 man**
Military Cross Awarded	**1 man**

The total cost of the force in 1919 was £2,197.15s.7d.

Traffic Problems 1920

This was the year when traffic problems began to rear their ugly head. The Chief Constable decided to place two men on traffic duty, one at the Nelson Place - Merrial Street junction and the other to be on duty at the junction of Bridge Street and Red Lion Square. These officers were to be on duty in the morning and evening to facilitate traffic. Only a few months later the Chief Constable was complaining about traffic congestion in Red Lion Square. Mr Forster said that the free flow of traffic was hindered by Hackney Carriages waiting and tramcars stopping to pick up and set down passengers.

Red Lion Square, Newcastle - scene of the first traffic congestion problems in the 1920's.

**Good Report from
HM Inspector
1920**

The force was again inspected in March 1920 by Major General Llewellyn Atcherley, HM Inspector of Constabulary, who remarked that he was pleased with all he had seen. Later in the year the Watch Committee received the usual certificate to say that the force had been kept in an efficient state for the preceding twelve months. Without this certificate the Council would not receive the 50% grant from the Home Office.

**Rent Allowance
Introduced
1920**

The Watch Committee decided in 1920 to pay to the force a Rent Allowance, as follows:

Unmarried constables	4/- per week
Married constables	6/6d per week
Sergeants	7/6d per week

The Chief Constable was to receive £40 per annum.

At this time, the officers were also to receive an allowance of 1/- per week to purchase batteries for their lamps.
The cost of the force had risen by nearly £900 in one year, to a total cost of £3,089.13s.10d.

**Proposal for
Amalgamation
1921**

In 1921, due to the increasing cost of the force, the Watch Committee received a communication from the Finance and General Purpose Committee of the Council, asking them to consider the taking over of the policing of the Borough by the County. The Town Clerk was instructed to write to the County authorities to ascertain their general terms, conditions and costs for policing the Borough. In the following month, the Watch Committee received a letter from the County authorities requesting more information. But the Watch Committee then decided that no further action be taken. The Borough force had escaped yet another attempt at a merger with its much larger neighbour!

The Chief Constable again complained of the excessive number of assaults on his men. He wrote to the Clerk of the Justices requesting that this information be passed on to the magistrates at their next meeting and that the situation be seriously considered.

It is interesting to note that at this time the Watch Committee still considered it part of their duty to inspect all items of police clothing before placing the tender each year.

**Cost Cutting
Starts!
1922**

Financial restrictions would appear to be nothing new. In March 1922, the Watch Committee received a letter from the Home Office stating that the committee of National Expenditure had been looking into the cost of the police forces and in view of this was asking all forces to suspend all recruiting and that any vacancies occurring through natural wastage - resignations, retirements or death - be left unfilled until further notice. The police were also instructed to turn off, at 11pm each night, the gas and water supplies to the two public conveniences situated in the town. The force did, however, make its first contribution at this time to the Clearing House for criminal information at Wakefield, run by the West Riding Constabulary.

The Chief Constable's annual reports refer again to the traffic congestion in the Borough caused mainly by motor vehicles, but it would appear that horses were still a problem, because PC Dutton received a commendation from the Watch Committee for his brave action in stopping a runaway horse in the town in May 1922.

PC Beeston made application to the Watch Committee asking that he be allowed to terminate the use of his house as a house of detention for children. His request was granted and the home of PC Wesley Bate at 25 Brindley Street was then offered and used on the same terms as previously granted to PC Beeston. Less than a year later PC Bate was to cease using his home. PC Mounse offered the use of his home at 3 Windsor Street. This was accepted by the committee.

Before the end of 1922, ex-PC Ford was to return to the fold, but

he was subjected to a twelve months probationary period, with the Police Surgeon reporting on his suitability for permanent employment within the force. He had originally joined the force in 1910, but due to injury received during the Great War he was not fit for police duty when he returned in 1919. A few weeks later the doctor reported that PC Ford was unable to perform the rigours of police duty expected of him. It is sad to speculate the difficulties that poor PC Ford was experiencing in finding gainful employement after his war injury!

Complaints and Congratulations 1922

At the April meeting of the Watch Committee two letters were read, one from the Library committee complaining about the constant theft of newspapers and magazines from the reading room in the free library. They were of the opinion that the police were not taking enough steps to alleviate the problem!

The second letter was from the directors of T W Carryers & Co, expressing thanks to the police for dealing with a fire that had occurred at their premises. They enclosed a cheque to the value of £2.8s.0d to pay for the fire extinguisher, with the remainder to be divided amongst those constables who had dealt with the fire. At that time Carryers' shop was situated opposite the Old Police Station.

In 1923 that the Automobile Association was granted permission to erect signs telling motorists that they could park their cars in the High Street, near to the Town Hall.

In December, the National Union of Shop Assistants complained to the Borough Council that the Shops Act was not being enforced. They urged the Watch Committee to call upon the Shops Inspector to take more effective action to enforce the half day closing. The Council sent a letter of reply to the Union, in which they said that they were quite satisfied that the Chief Constable was enforcing the act in a satisfactory manner.

Before the year closed a duplicating machine was purchased for the police office from the Luton Typewriting and Office Supplies. The cost of the machine is not recorded.

**Royal Visit
1924**

The town was honoured by a Royal Visit when the Prince of Wales visited the borough in 1924. At this time the actual strength of the Borough force was 21 men, two less than the authorised establishment of 23. To help with crowd control, 35 men were loaned from the Stoke-on-Trent force and a similar number from the County. Both police authorities waived all charges. The Watch Committee also sent a letter of thanks to Sir Robert Peacock, Chief Constable of Manchester, for the loan of street barriers.

The Police uniforms for 1924 were purchased from John Hammond & Co of Newcastle at a cost of £103.6s.6d.

In October, the Chief Constable applied to the Watch Committee for permission to fill the two vacancies. In the statement which he placed before the committee he said,

"I have to find two men for traffic points each day and an area of the Westlands has been added to the Borough and I have to say that I am not able to police the town as efficiently as I would wish with the number of men available to me."

Mr Forster must have proved his case for his request was granted.

The police surgeon, Dr Cauldwell, received an increase in his pay and allowances before the year was out. He was to be paid £25 per year to supply surgical and medical cover to members of the force and prisoners, and to medically examine potential candidates. He was also paid for attending street accidents - 7/6d by day and 10/6d at night. For inspecting boys and girls who were to be sent to Reformatory School he was to be paid 10/6d.

The total cost to run the force for 1924 was £3,447.8s.3d.

The year 1925 seems to have been a quiet one for the Borough police. The Chief Constable reported that out of 18 men taking the promotion examination, 14 passed in all subjects.

The Watch Committee agreed to the Pavilion Cinema opening on Good Friday, providing that the film to be shown had been approved by the Chief Constable. Not the kind of censorship which would be deemed acceptable today!

General Strike 1926

The Chief Constable reported to the Watch Committee in April 1926 that there had been no serious trouble in the town during the General Strike. A large number of Special Constables were sworn in but their services were not required. The St John's Ambulance Brigade were put on standby and they manned the ambulance throughout the strike because the police were committed to other duties.

Honour for Chief Constable Forster 1926

Mr Forster was elected President of the Chief Constable's Association in June 1926. The Mayor said at the Council meeting that it was not only an honour for the Chief Constable, but the whole town.

In January the Chief Constable had received a circular from the Home Office, in which they they emphasised the growing importance of police officers possessing a thorough knowledge of first aid. The Chief Constable formed a class and PC Hawley volunteered to be the instructor. In May sixteen members of the force passed the examination. To show their appreciation all members of the class subscribed to a silver cigarette case and presented it to PC Hawley, who also trained eleven members of the Fire Brigade. Twelve months later Mr Forster was able to report that every member of the force now possessed the First Aid Certificate.

In 1926 a new typewriter was purchased at a cost of £24. It replaced one which had been in use since 1913. In the following months electric lights were fixed in the cells.

Motoring Accidents Increase Driving Licences Proposed 1927

In his report for 1917, the Chief Constable, Mr Forster, referred to the enormous increase in road accidents over the past five years, and he may have been instrumental in the decision to send the following letter to the Home Office:

"The council of this Borough are concerned about the dangers of granting driving licenses to people who are young or incompetent through disability, and we suggest that all persons be examined prior to the issuing of a driving licence. We urge the Home Office to take steps to pass the necessary legislation."

Five years later, the 'necessary legislation' was indeed passed by the Government.

On 14th July two civilians rendered good service when they captured a prisoner who had escaped while being conveyed to the Police Station. Both men were awarded £1.1s.0d by the Watch Committee. At the same time, PCs Phillips and Rutter were commended by the Watch Committee for stopping runaway horses in the town.

Increase in the Area of Borough 1927

On the last day of October 1927, the area of the Borough was increased by 900 acres, when Clayton and part of the Westlands were added to it. To help with the policing of the enlarged area, three additional constables were appointed, the first increase in strength since 1914 and this brought the authorised strength of the force to twenty six.

In May 1927 the force was inspected by C de Courcy Parry CBE, HM Inspector of Constabulary. In November the Watch Committee received the usual certificate from the Home Office. With effect from 1st February 1928 the police were advised that, on notification of a fire they were to call the Fire Brigade immediately and then proceed to the scene and attempt to extinguish the fire. Prior to this date members of the force would, on receiving notification of a fire, proceed to the scene with hand extinguishers kept at the Police Office, and if they were not able to put out the fire, the Brigade had only then been called.

In the same month the Mayor and Chief Constable attended a meeting at Hyde for the purpose of discussing the question of the government proposal to abolish the small borough forces. It was to take another nineteen years for this move to come to fruition.

PC James Guest had only been a member of the force for four months when, in April 1928, he was knocked down by a car whilst directing traffic in Nelson Place. He was off work for 28 days and the driver was fined £10 plus costs for "driving to the common danger".

At the annual inspection of the force in November, HM Inspector recommended that a matron be appointed for night duty. Mrs Elsie Beeston, daughter of the Matron, was appointed. She was paid £2 per annum plus five shillings per night when she was called out.

**Eight Hour
Continuous Shifts
Requested
1929**

The constables placed an application before the Watch Committee in February 1929 in which they requested an eight hour shift system of continual duty. Up to this time the day duty had consisted of two four hour shifts. Only the night duty had been performed in one continuous eight hour shift. The Watch Committee conceded to this request, initially for an experimental period of twelve months, at the end of which it was made permanent.

**Meritorious
Conduct**

In June, the Watch Committee received a letter from Police Surgeon, Dr Cauldwell, in praise of the meritorious conduct of PC A Burrow. The constable had administered artificial respiration to a man who had attempted suicide by coal gas poisoning. Had PC Burrow not acted so efficiently the man would not have survived, said the doctor.

In April 1930, the Chief Constable reported a case of meritorious action by a Mr George Burke of 6, Froghall, Newcastle. Mr Forster's report states that:

"At 5pm on 26th March a lorry with no driver and ineffi-cient brakes ran away down Froghall towards Lower Street. At the time a number of children were playing in the street and Burke, who had his own child in his arms, managed to push three of the children out of the way. One girl was unfortunately struck by the wheel of the lorry and died later in the Royal Infirmary at Stoke."

Burke was awarded the customary £1.1s.0d by the Watch Committee.

The Chief Constable had a pay increase in 1930 which raised his pay from £354 to £404 per annum. In 1930 the force cost £4,316 to run, against £3,089 in 1920.

**Traffic Problems
First
Traffic Lights
1931**

Traffic seemed to be the main problem for both the police and the Council at this time. 1931 saw the erection of the first set of automatic traffic lights in the town, at the junction of Merrial Street and High Street, and the roadway by the Guildhall and the old police station was made into a one way street. Twelve months later the roundabout in Nelson Place was built to facilitate the flow of traffic at this busy road junction.

In December 1931, considerable interest was shown in a case brought under the licensing act, which was heard at the Borough Police Court. It seems that on Mayor's Sunday, a number of councillors and other dignitaries had accompanied the Mayor to St Giles Church, but only as far as the gateway. They then left the procession and proceeded to the Talbot Hotel opposite, where they were later discovered by Sergeant Cotton and PC Naylor, drinking during prohibited hours. Thirty two persons appeared  before the court, including a number of councillors. The fines ranged from £20 for the landlord to 7/6d for the imbibers.

The Chief Constable in his annual report for the year said that there were 97 licensed premises in the Borough.

Large Increase in Borough Area and Force 1932

This year saw the biggest change in the Borough Police force since its formation almost one hundred years previously. On 1st April 1932, the Wolstanton United Urban District Council, which embraced the mining villages of Chesterton, Silverdale and Knutton, became part of the Borough of Newcastle-under-Lyme, doubling the population of the town overnight as the area increased from 1,756 acres to 8,882 acres. The force had to be increased in strength from 26 to 55 men. At the time of this merger, the Wolstanton area was being policed by the Staffordshire County Police and certain members of the new Council thought that the County should continue to police the enlarged Borough area, principally because it would be more economical. The Chairman of the Watch Committee, Alderman Beresford said, *"I and the people of Newcastle are very proud of our force. H M Inspectors have always spoken very highly of it, and I think we should keep it"*.

Chief Constable William Forster, photographed in Keele Road, 1922.
Author's collection

Welcome to Greater Newcastle - members of Staffordshire County Constabulary who have been transferred to the Newcastle Borough Force, being welcomed by the Mayor of Newcastle the Rt Hon Colonel J C Wedgwood DSO, MP, JP. On the right is Mr G W Hoon, a member of the new Town Council and Chairman of the Wolstanton Council which it has now superceded.

County Police who had served in the Wolstanton area and who were transferred to the Borough Force on 1st April 1932 when the Borough was enlarged, are seen here receiving their helmets from Sgt. Wesley Bate, the Chief Clerk.   *S entinel*

Alderman Beresford won the day and and three sergeants and thirteen constables transferred from the Newcastle Division of the County force to the Borough on the 1st April 1932. One inspector, one sergeant and six constables were kept on loan from the County and were expected to remain so until June.

Ten new constables were also sworn in and sent to the Police Training School at Birmingham, being the first members of the Borough force to receive such formal training. Up to this time any training had been done on the job, with a guidance from the senior men and the sergeant.

Death of Chief Constable Forster 1932

On 13th April 1932, members of the force received the sad news that their Chief Constable of the last twenty years, Mr Forster, had died in the City General Hospital, Stoke-on-Trent, at the age of 62 years. Mr Forster had been ill for some weeks. Owing to the Chief Constable's indisposition during his illness, quite a lot of the planning of the merger had been undertaken by Sergeant Wesley Bate, the Chief Clerk. At the meeting of the Watch Committee at the end of April, to show their appreciation, the committee promoted Mr Bate to Inspector and made him Acting Chief Constable. Later, in July, he was awarded £64.11s.6d for his time as Acting Chief Constable and promoted to Chief Inspector.

Chief Constable George Sidney Lowe 1932 - 1936

On Wednesday 1st June 1932 the Watch Committee interviewed twelve applicants for the vacant post of Chief Constable. The successful applicant was George Sidney Lowe, who at that time was Chief Constable of Congleton Borough Police, Cheshire. He took up his duties on 18th June, as the fifteenth Chief Constable of the Borough. Mr Lowe had joined the Newcastle-on-Tyne City Police in 1913, left to serve in the Great War and then rejoined the force in 1918. He left Newcastle-on-Tyne on promotion to inspector at Scarborough and was appointed Chief Constable of Congleton in 1930. His salary was to be £550 rising to £700 per annum after nine years.

The Chief Constable set about his task of policing the enlarged Borough with vigour. A cycle patrol of three sergeants and nine constables was established to cover the outlying area of the town.

The funeral of Chief Constable Mr Wm. Forster was held at St Giles Church, Newcastle on 15th April 1932. On the right hand side of the picture can be seen a contingent of Staffordshire County Policemen and on the left a contingent of men from the Stoke on Trent force. *Author's collection*

H M Inspectors Parade, 1933. H M Inspector Lt Col Allan and Chief Constable G S Lowe. *John Naylor*

A cycle was also purchased for the sole use of the CID, along with photographic equipment and a new rotary duplicator.

Re-organisation of CID 1933

Less than twelve months later the CID was reorganised. Two constables were sent on a Detective Training Course, one to Wakefield with the West Riding force and the other to the Warwickhire Constabulary. PC Hobson, who had himself just returned from a similar course at Birmingham, was promoted to Sergeant and placed in charge of the department. Detective Sergeant Nother, who had been on a CID course at Scotland Yard, was to replace Hobson in April 1935.

The cost of the Crime Information Reports received from the West Riding Constabulary went up from £7.5s.0d per year to £16.3s.0d.

The wives of four of the constables were acting as matrons at this time. They were paid 1/- per hour when engaged. A woman was also employed to clean the Police Station, for which she received 12/6d per week.

John Edward Carter was appointed as boy clerk in the office, on the understanding that he joined the force when he came of age. He was the son of Mr Roger Carter, Chief Constable of Stoke-on-Trent.

Mr Lowe was the first Chief Constable of the Borough to be supplied with an official car. He was also the first Chief Constable to live in the Police House at 1 Priory Road, built at the cost of £1,370.

The year closed with the strength and cost of the force as follows:

Chief Constable 1   **£500 to £700 plus allowances.**
Chief Inspector 1   **£365 to £405 per annum**

Inspectors	2	£310 to £350 per annum
Sergeants	7	100/- to 112/6d per week
Constables	44	Per national regulations

Inspector Fullerton and Sergeant Bradley were the last two members of the County Police to return to their own force, leaving the Borough in November.

1932 was also to see the end of the ornate helmet worn by members of the Borough force since 1889, replaced by Home Office standard pattern issue.

Inadequate Police Stations 1934

Now that the Chief Constable had reorganised the force, his next priority was to get the Council to build him a new station. The present station had been in use since 1834 and had only ever received the most minor alterations. It was obvious that the station was totally inadequate as the headquarters of the new enlarged force.

The force had also taken possession of four small County stations, situated at Chesterton, Silverdale, Wolstanton and 66 and 68 Oxford Street, Basford. The Council immediately spent £529 on repairs and improvements to these four stations.

In December 1934 the accommodation for single men was moved from the Silverdale station to the station at Chesterton, because the Chief Constable considered the Silverdale station unsuitable. No expense was spared by the Council when they allocated the princely sum of £5 to refurbish a room which accommodated five single men. Two years later fifteen pounds was spent on the Silverdale station to try and alleviate the problem with damp. In 1936, at the Sanitary Inspector's insistence, the resident sergeant was moved out to alternative accommodation. The Watch Committee then instructed the Sanitary Inspector and the Borough Surveyor to inspect the stations at Chesterton and Silverdale and submit a report, which was received some months later. It recommended that both stations should be replaced. (It would appear that the Council did not pay too much attention to this report because in 1936, they invested £31.19s.0d in the replacement of the gas lighting with electric).

Meter Robberies a Problem

One of the main problems concerning the force at this time was the number of gas and electricity meters being raided.

The Police Surgeon was now to be paid £75 per annum due to his additional work load.

Chief Superintendent Richards of the Newcastle Division of the County force was still acting as Inspector under the Petroleum Act for the Wolstanton area of the Borough nine months after the merger! Mr Richards sent in his claim for £15 as entitled but the Council decided to pay only £10 to him and his job as Petroleum Inspector was terminated forthwith.

The Chief Constable reported to the Watch Committee and requested and was granted, permission to sell a considerable amount of almost new saddlery in stock that would not be required in the future.

The boot allowance of £2.12s.0d per year was cancelled and instead the men were to be issued with boots. This was instigated at the suggestion of the Chief Constable in the interests of uniformity. Less than twelve months later the issue of boots was to be stopped and the boot allowance reinstated.
The Chief Constable also asked the Watch Committee to purchase an oxygen apparatus which was to be kept at the Police Station and used to revive asphyxiated persons. The apparatus cost £3.15s.0d.

Chief Constable's Report 1935

The Watch Committee was notified of a communication received from the Home Office, informing the Chief Constable that all police personnel were to receive training in fire fighting, which would enable them to commence fire fighting before the Fire Brigade arrived, should they happen to arrive first on the scene. Inspector Lewis had returned from Birmingham after receiving training and was now ready to instruct other members of the force in their new duty. In 1935, the Chief Officer of the Fire Brigade was to take over this duty.

The Chief Constable complained to the Watch Committee that he

Laying the Foundation Stone of the new Police Station. Merrial Street 4th March 1935

Funeral of Chief Inspector Joseph Burrow at St Giles Church, 11th March 1942. Note that the men are carrying their gas masks.   *Insp D Baldwin*

did not possess a sword and that on occasions when he was required to wear full dress uniform, he was obliged to borrow one. Regulations required that he wear one when in full dress uniform. He was given authorisation to purchase a sword and scabbard.

The Chief Constable received a memo from the Home Office relating to the standardisation of police uniform throughout England and Wales.

On the Chief Constable's recommendation, the Watch Committee brought in a compulsory retirement rule after thirty years of service.

Stray Dogs Causing traffic accidents

One of the main causes of road traffic accidents in the Borough, according to the Chief Constable's report for 1935, was too many dogs not under proper control, There were far too many dogs roaming the streets, he said.

Royal Review of Police Forces July 1935

Four constables were to represent the Borough force at the review of police forces to be held in London's Hyde Park on 20th July 1935, before His Majesty King George V. One inspector and one sergeant, along with the Chief Constable, attended as spectators.

In July, the Chief Constable received a memo from the Home Office relating to air raid precautions - it was to be the first of many!

Women PCs Proposed

The Watch Committee received a letter from the National Council of Women of Great Britain, in which they asked the Watch Committee to consider the appointment of women police officers in the town. The committee decided to take no action.

Uniform clothing for the year cost £353.12s.4d, and for the first time the white metal buttons which had hitherto been on the uniform great coats were replaced by black ones.

Opening of New Headquarters Merrial Street 1936

The Chief Constable saw his plans come to fruition on 29th February 1936, when the new Police Headquarters in Merrial Street were opened by Sir Llewelyn Atcherly, CMG, CVO, HM Inspector of Constabulary, who deputised for Mr A L Dixon CB, CBE, Assistant secretary for the Home Office, who was indisposed.

The H M Inspector said that twenty seven years had elapsed since a new police station had first been suggested. This station replaced one that had been in use since 1st November 1834, the day the force was established.

Telephone Pillars Introduced

To coincide with the opening of the new station, the police telephone and signalling system also came into use. 36 GPO telephone pillars, each with a light on top which, when switched on, would attract the attention of constables on the beat when they were required by headquarters, were placed at various points throughout the Borough. The police pillar and signalling system had been agreed by the Home Office, providing that the force was kept one man below establishment!

The total cost of the new station, including fixtures, fittings, telephone system, etc., was £25,200. The Fire Brigade Committee agreed to contribute fifty guineas per annum towards the rental of the police pillars. These pillars, for which the Council paid a yearly rental, remained the property of the Postmaster General.

Chief Constable Lowe Leaves Borough 1936

Mr Lowe was not to remain long in his new police headquarters. He left Newcastle on 22nd March 1936, to take up the post of Chief Constable of Plymouth. The Watch Committee placed on record its appreciation of the services of Mr G S Lowe over the previous four years. The following letter was sent by the Chief Constable to the Watch Committee:

> *Chief Constable's Office*
> *Borough Police*
> *Newcastle, Staffs*
> *19th March 1936*

Dear Mr Mayor
I would like to express to you and each member of the Watch Committee, before leaving for Plymouth, my sincere thanks and appreciation of the many kindnesses shown by you during my period of service here as Chief Constable.
The high standard of efficiency in the police service today is due largely to your sympathetic interest and loyal support in all matters where the welfare of the force has been concerned and the organisation is one of which you can be truly proud.

The Borough Force taken at the opening of the new police station in Merrial Street, 1936. Chief Constable is G S Lowe.

Author's collection

Front Row: H Chambers, B Wright, Sgt J Jones, Sgt L Hobson, Sgt C Lawton, Insp. Burrows, Chief Insp.W Bates, CC G S Lowe, Insp. Lewis, Sgt Albert Skinner, Sgt G Swetenham, Sgt Poynton, B Byatt, S L Durrent, J W Woolley.

Middle Row: D G Cooper CID, E Carter, F NMorris, B Morris, E W Mawson, L Chadwick, J Guest, F Norcup, B Watts, W R Gripton, G N Powis E Greensill, G W Mills, PC Birtwhistle, PC Willson, W Gray, Insp. Nother CID.

Back Row: J Monford, G Moore, G A Rutter, T Bird, H Bennett, J B Thornthwait, W Roper, I R Cogbill, L T H Pullman, Bruce Robb, H E S Gibson, R Hazell, C Naylor.

In Caps: W E Dunn, D Graham

The Old Police Station was in use from 1834 until 1936, when the force moved into the new station in Merrial Street. The Old Station occupied the site of what is now the Lancaster Buildings.

Author's collection

Merrial Street Police Station during WW2. Note the sandbags placed around the station.

Author's collection

I am certain you will be well served by Mr Bate and I trust he will be accorded the support, loyalty and friendship which you gave me unstintingly.

With very kind regards,
Very sincerely yours,
G S Lowe, Chief Constable.

Chief Constable
Wesley Bate
1936 - 1943

At the meeting of the Watch Committee held on 17th March 1936, it was decided not to advertise the vacancy of Chief Constable but to offer it to Chief Inspector Wesley Bate, a man known and respected not only by members of the Watch Committee and police force but also by most of the townspeople. The choice proved very popular. Wesley Bate was born in New Zealand, where his father was employed as a railway engineer. Soon after Wesley's birth his family returned to England and settled in Wolverhampton, where young Wesley attended Wolverhampton High School and gained two scholarships. He joined the Borough force in May 1911 and after a short period on street duty he was appointed Clerk. When the Great War broke out he volunteered for the Army. On his return in October 1919, he resumed his duties as clerk. He was promoted sergeant in April 1924, inspector in April 1932 and chief inspector three months later.

The Chief Constable was authorised to purchase one standard uniform from Enderley Mills at a cost of £7.10s.0d and one full dress uniform at a cost of £11.11s.0d.

Constable George Shaw was bitten by a dog when on duty in the town in September. The town clerk informed the Watch Committee meeting that he was trying to recover from the owner of the dog the pay and allowances of the constable whilst he was off duty, plus all out of pocket expenses. There is no record that he was successful.

The force appointed the first female clerk telephone operator. She was to be paid £65 per annum.

Vandalism again
1937

In 1937 vandalism in the Wolstanton and Porthill areas of the Borough was causing concern. The Parks department reported damage to trees, etc. on Wolstanton Marsh and householders

**Complaints about
Service to the
New Areas
1937**

complained of damage to their fences and hedges. Residents of the area said that there were no policemen about and that the Wolstanton police station was not always open.

One councillor remarked that he knew of someone who had to travel all the way to Newcastle to produce his driving licence. The same councillor said that there were over 20,000 people living in the area and that the police station should be open at all times. The Chief Constable replied that stationed at Wolstanton there were nine constables and one resident sergeant, which represented an increase of four men since the time when it had been a County station. There were also eight police pillars in the area and it was also regularly visited by the motor patrol by day and night. Mr Bate said that if the station were manned twenty four hours per day the people of Silverdale and Chesterton would expect the same, which would be impossible at the force's present strength.

All these complaints doubtless provided valuable ammunition for the Chief Constable to fire at the Watch Committee a few months later, when he was to seek an increase of ten men to bring his force up to a strength of 65 men. In his report Mr Bate provided the following information:

> *Newcastle had the highest ratio of population and acreage per officer of any of the twenty seven other boroughs with the same population with 1,177 persons and 161.5 acres to one officer. There were also five miles of main road and twenty schools in the Borough. There were twenty four traffic points that needed manning for children on their way to and from school. After taking into account office staff, motor patrol, CID and leave and sickness, there were only eleven uniform men left on duty at any one time.*
>
> *The Chief Constable then accused the council of running the force on the cheap. He agreed to try and manage with ten extra men but, if this proved impossible he would return once more to the committee. In October the Home Office sent a letter confirming their agreement to the increase in the force size.*

1938: PC Lester in winter uniform.

Policeman using a police telephone pillar. 35 of these pillars were erected at various locations within the Borough. If the police station wanted to contact the patrol constable the light on top of the pillar was activated.
Sgt. Ian Bentley

1938: Chief Constable Bate photographed during the Mayor's Parade. *Sentinel*

Coronation of King George V1 1937

The Chief Constable received an invitation to attend the Coronation of King George VI at Westminster Abbey on 12th May 1937. Chief Inspector Burrow was to act in the Chief Constable's absence. PC William Byatt, who was the senior constable in the force, was awarded the Coronation Medal and retired the following month after 26 years service.

Preparations for War Begin again 1937

Preparations for war were getting underway again. Chief Inspector Burrow had returned from an instructor's course on anti-gas measures. All the other members of the Borough police then received anti-gas training, carried out in conjunction with the City Police at Stoke.

The Chief Constable was given authority to recruit up to 100 special constables. Only men over 40 years of age were to be considered, except in exceptional circumstances.

At the October meeting of the Watch Committee, Councillor Haywood asked the Chief Constable about his intentions regarding a Home Office memo sent to all forces suggesting that loud speakers be fitted to all police cars. Mr Bate replied that he thought they were *"looking too far into the future"*, but Councillor Haywood disagreed, replying that *"I think it should be looked into. They will be most useful, especially in case of air raids, and we will get a grant off the Home Office."*

Pit Disaster at Holditch Colliery 1937

In July 1937, thirty men perished in a disaster at Brymbo Pit - later known as Holditch Colliery, Chesterton. The Borough Council sent a letter of thanks to the Chief Constable of Stoke-on-Trent and also to the Chief Fire officer of the City, thanking them for their help on the occasion of the explosion.

At the close of 1937 the authorised strength of the force was 65, but the actual strength was 57. The new establishment of the force was made up as follows:

    1 **Chief Constable**
    1 **Chief Inspector**
    2 **Inspectors**
    8 **Sergeants**
  53 **Constables**

New Police Stations 1938

New sectional stations were built in Wolstanton Road, Chesterton and Church Lane, Knutton in 1938. The old station at Chesterton was vacated and the Silverdale station, which was a terraced house, was sold. The cost of the new stations was in total £1,431.4s.0d - just over £700 each.

The telephone system at the Newcastle station was improved when three additional outside lines were installed, together with seven internal extensions and a private line to the Staffordshire County Police Station in Water Street.

In October, the licensee of the Rainbow Public house in Newcastle, which stood opposite the old police station in High Street, was charged with taking bets. PC Bates of the Stoke-on-Trent City Police gave evidence, stating that he had kept the premises under observation, wearing plain clothes. It would appear that the constable had been on loan from the city force for this surveillance work, presumably because the local force, being so small, would all have been known to the licensee and his customers. PC Bates was stationed with the Longton Division of the City Police, the division which was furthest away from Newcastle.

Rise in Crime Figures

In his annual report, Mr Bate listed 241 indictable offences committed, as against a total of 196 for the previous year. Cases of simple larceny had risen from 45 to 104 cases, children being responsible for 41 of them. Road accidents revealed a decrease, with the black spot being at Porthill Bank, where 15 accidents had been reported.

Police Reserve 1939

The year opened with the Chief Constable reporting that the Home Office had sanctioned the number of the First Police Reserve for the Borough, which was not to exceed ten men. Mr Bate added that he had six former members of the force who were willing to serve and that each man would receive a retainer fee of £5 per annum. The Watch Committee decided to take no further action on the matter for the present.

Still no Place for Women PCs

Later in the year the Chief Constable informed a meeting of the Watch Committee that he did not, at this stage, propose to recruit women for police duty.

PC L Chadwick wearing 1930's style of uniform. *Mrs Chadwick*

PC Clarence Naylor photographed in dress uniform. This uniform was discontinued in 1932 *John Naylor*

PC L Chadwick wearing WW 2 uniform with tin helmet. *Mrs Chadwick*

Special Constable Wilmot Sedgeley. Killed by enemy action in WW2.
Mrs Cummings, - daughter

The Chief Constable true to his word, in April 1939 placed before the Watch Committee his request for ten additional men, made up of eight constables, one sergeant and one inspector. The application was submitted to the Home Office, along with the Chief Constable's report, and the Home Office acceded to the request.The force was now distributed as follows:

	1	**Chief Constable**
	1	**Chief Inspector**
	3	**Inspectors**
	2	**Constable Clerk**
CID	1	**Detective Sergeant**
	2	**Detective Constables**
	1	**Constable Clerk CID**
	1	**Constable, Coroner's Office**
Patrol	8	**Sergeants**
	<u>52</u>	**Constables**
Total	<u>75</u>	

A pay increase was awarded to the Chief Constable with effect from 1st January, which would take his maximum pay from £700 to £800 per annum.

Outbreak of Second World War 1939

On Sunday 3rd September 1939, Sergeant Leonard Hobson was promoted to Inspector bringing the establishment of Inspectors to three. PC Clarence Naylor was promoted sergeant. From that day the police force, along with all other establishments in Britain, went onto a war footing. Precautions had already been taken against the fateful day and the force was well prepared. £100 had been spent on blackout covering for the windows at Newcastle and Wolstanton Police Stations. The roof and the floors at the

BOROUGH OF NEWCASTLE-UNDER-LYME.

POLICE NOTICE.

PUBLIC AIR RAID SHELTERS

This SHELTER is provided for the protection of the GENERAL PUBLIC during an Air Raid and must not be used for any unlawful purpose.

NOTICE IS HEREBY GIVEN - that any person found committing any Nuisance or Wilfully Damaging this Property or Protecting Materials will be prosecuted.

By Order,

W. BATE,

Chief Constable's Office, Newcastle-under-Lyme.

Chief Constable.

G. T. Bagguley, Printer, Newcastle.

Newcastle Station were also strengthened and sandbags placed outside the station as a precaution against bomb blast. Eighteen months later the sandbags were replaced by a blast wall.

Four members of the force who were Army Reservists were

Sgt. F Norcup seen here with evacuees in King Street Newcastle c 1940.   *Sentinel*

recalled to join their regiments.

The year 1940, opened with the Chief Constable receiving a Home Office circular relating to the issue of uniform advising him to suspend the annual issue only replacing essential items.

In June, the Chief Constable informed the Watch Committee that he had received information from the Home Office to set the maximum number of full time auxiliaries employed by the force at 35, this figure to include 15 War Reservists.

Newcastle Struck by Enemy Bombs 1940

The first bomb to fall in North Staffordshire, on July 26th 1940, hit a house in Gower Street, Newcastle, killing a young boy who had only arrived from London as an evacuee on the previous day. Before the year was over enemy bombers again attacked the Borough and two weeks before Christmas bombs were dropped on Chesterton, killing fourteen people. A small detachment of Borough policemen were sent to Coventry to assist during and after the terrible blitzing of that city.

Special Constable killed by Enemy Bomb 1941

German raiders were to strike North Staffordshire yet again on the night of 16th January, 1941, when bombs were dropped on the Basford area of the town in Downing Avenue. A number of members of the Regular and Special Constabulary were soon on the scene helping to search for survivors. Whilst this work was in progress a bomb with a delayed action exploded, killing Special Constable Wilmot Sedgeley and injuring several other officers, one seriously. Mr Sedgeley left a widow and two young children.

First Radio Communication 1941

Radio - (or wireless, as it was then known) communication was adopted by the Borough force in June 1941. Receiving sets were fixed in the two patrol cars and a third set placed in the main Police Station. The system was owned and operated by the Stoke-on-Trent City police, but Newcastle contributed to the cost of setting up the system, which totalled £112.10s.0d.

Two years later the wireless communication became two-way, which meant that the three patrol cars now fitted with radio were able to transmit as well as receive messages. The Chief Constable of Stoke-on-Trent suggested that Newcastle's Watch Committee should contribute one fifth of the annual cost.

**Young Vandals
hit Train!
Offenders Birched!
1941**

A train crowded with passengers was endangered by the pranks of five small boys between 8 and 12 years of age, when they placed a platelayers' trolley on the line in the vicinity of the railway crossing at Knutton. A train approaching from the Silverdale direction ran into the trolley, smashing it to pieces, causing slight damage to the engine. Fortunately there were no injuries to passengers. When they appeared before Newcastle Juvenile Court three of the boys were ordered to receive four strokes of the birch and one to receive three strokes. After the decision to birch the boys had been taken the Chief Constable, Mr Wesley Bate made a formal protest against the police being asked to administer the birch to the boys, but the Magistrates' Clerk pointed out that the law stated that birching must be carried out by a constable in the presence of a police officer of high rank.

**Sudden Death of
Chief Inspector
Burrow
1942**

The entire force was saddened to learn of the death of Chief Inspector Burrow on Saturday 7th March 1942, in the North Staffordshire Royal Infirmary, a few days before his 48th birthday. Mr Burrow was a native of Westlinton, Cumbria and had joined the Borough force in 1914. The following year he had enlisted in the army, returning to his police duties in September 1919. His funeral took place at St Giles Church, Newcastle.

In April, the Committee received a memo from the Home Office, asking that economy measures be exercised over consumption of petrol. A few days later a second memo was received by the Watch Committee, informing them that the Home Office would have the power to authorise the retirement of any Chief Constable without consulting the local authority!

At the end of May 1942, the Chief Constable had returned to duty, having been on extended leave due to illness since January. With effect from 1st June all policemen under the age of 25 and auxiliaries under the age of 30 became eligible for military service. Mr Bate announced that this would affect 15 regular officers but no members of the auxiliary service.

Colonel J de Coke CMG, CVO, CBE, HM Inspector of Constabulary, inspected the force under working conditions in

June. He expressed his pleasure at what he had seen. Inspector Lewis was promoted to Chief Inspector in September, filling the vacancy left by the death of Mr Burrow.

Government Proposals for Amalgamation 1942

In October, the Town Clerk received a letter from the Association of Municipal Corporations, pointing out that the Home Secretary had made a statement in Parliament relating to the amalgamation of the police forces of all non-county borough councils.

Resignation of Chief Constable Mr Wesley Bate 1943

In February 1943 Mr Bate tendered his resignation, due to ill health. He had been a member of the Borough force since 1911 and Chief Constable since 1936. The Watch Committee asked Mr Bate to reconsider his decision but he refused, due to the state of his health. The committee placed on record the devoted manner in which the Chief Constable had discharged his duty, also the efficient state in which he had always maintained the force.

From 60 applicants for his replacement, a shortlist of 14 was drawn up for interview:

A L Clarke	Superintendent, Stoke-on-Trent
A C Clements	Chief Inspector, Birmingham
D H Burns	Inspector, Dudley
C F Beale	Chief Constable, Penzance
G Parfitt	Superintendent, Oldham
R W Priest	Chief Constable, Bacup
G S Jackson	Superintendent, Hull
R Barnes	Chief Inspector, Nottingham
W Weatherhogg	Chief Constable, Grantham
H N Martyn	Chief Inspector, Lancashire County
L Hobson	Inspector, Newcastle-under-Lyme
H Chambers	Inspector, Newcastle-under-Lyme
A Skinner	Inspector, Newcastle-under-Lyme
E J Nother	Sergeant C I D Newcastle-under-Lyme

Chief Constable George Spencer Jackson OBE 1943 - 1946

Mr George Spencer Jackson took up his position as the Borough's 17th Chief Constable in May 1943. Although he had no way of knowing it at the time, subsequent events were also to make him the Borough's last Chief Constable.

Mr Wesley Bate, Chief Constable from 1936-43, photographed here during his time as Chief Inspector. Note that there are only two Bath Stars for Chief Inspector; also the black braid on the peak of the cap. At this time Inspectors in the borough wore only one Bath Star and did not have braid on the cap.

Author's collection

Chief Inspector Joseph Burrow, who acted as Mr Bate's Deputy from 1936-42. Inspector Burrow died in March 1942. *Inspector D Baldwin*

Death of Chief Inspector Burrow

North Staffordshire has lost a highly-esteemed and efficient police officer by the deeply regretted death, on Saturday night, of Chief Inspector Joseph Alfred Burrow, of the Newcastle Borough Constabulary.

Not only to his colleagues of the Borough Police and those of adjoining Forces, but to the general public, his passing has come as a great shock. He underwent an operation in the Royal Infirmary last Tues-

Inspector Burrow, c1933. Note the embroidered cap badge and the silver braid on the peak of the cap. *Sentinel*

Born in Sunderland, Mr Jackson joined Hull City Police in 1923, was promoted to sergeant in 1929, inspector in 1932 and superintendent in 1939. This was the first time that the appointment of the Borough's Chief Constable had to be approved by the Home Office, even though the Home Office had possessed this power over the appointment of County Chief Constables since 1856. A list of all applicants and all persons interviewed had to be forwarded for perusal by the Home Office.

The new Chief Constable spent £103.10s.0d on new equipment for the CID and private telephone lines were also installed to the three sectional stations at Wolstanton, Chesterton and Knutton.

PC 29 Harry (Jack) Jolly was awarded the RSPCA Bronze Medal and Certificate for his part in the rescue of a dog from a marl hole at Wolstanton in March 1943.

Officers serving with HM Forces were to be paid their increments when they fell due. Payments would be retrospective from the time they joined the forces.

The Watch Committee sent a letter to Mr A H Richardson upon his retirement as Chief Constable of Halifax. He had previously served at Newcastle. The committee received the following reply:

County Borough of Halifax Police Headquarters
Harrison Road
Halifax Yorks.

The Town Clerk,   *18th October 1943*
Town Clerk's Office,
Newcastle-under-Lyme.

Dear Mr Town Clerk
I very much appreciate the kind recollections and good wishes of your council and of yourself on the occasion of my retirement.
The war has caused me to remain in the police service a few

Inspector A Skinner, 1943.
Courtesy Miss Pat Skinner

Eileen Lawton in the uniform of the WAPC,
Newcastle Borough, 1942. Eileen was one of
the first two Women's Auxiliary Police
Officers appointed in Newcastle under Lyme
during the war years.   *Staffordshire Police*

years longer than I had intended and after so many years of official activity I shall welcome release from responsibilities.

With thanks again for your generous remembrances.

Yours faithfully

Alfred H Richardson

PC Robinson Graig killed on Active Service 1943

In November 1943 the Chief Constable reported the death of Police Constable Robinson Graig on active service. PC Graig was the only member of the regular force to lose his life on active service in the Second World War.

Reorganisation of the CID took place at the beginning of 1944 and to coincide with this, Detective Sergeant Nother was promoted to inspector and remained in charge of the department.

The Chief Constable said that in collaboration with the officer commanding the Newcastle and Kidsgrove wing of the Air Training Corps, he had formed a Police Auxiliary Messenger Service. The boys were all volunteers and would be used only in the event of an air raid. They would wear their own uniform and use their own bicycles. They would each be issued with a waterproof cape and a pair of leggings.

Questions were asked at the June 1944 meeting of the Watch Committee, when the Chief Constable reported that he was going to permit Inspector Skinner to retire. One member of the committee demanded to know why Inspector Skinner was to be granted that privilege when only a month previously the Chief Constable had refused to let a sergeant retire. The same member remarked that the Chief Constable of the County would not let his men retire during the present emergency under any circumstances.

Inspector Skinner had completed 32 years of service. Only six months later Chief Inspector Lewis, the Deputy Chief Constable, sort permission to retire, having completed 35 years of service, but his request was refused.

Sergeant Benjamin Wright was promoted to Inspector to fill the vacancy left by Mr Skinner. Inspector Wright had originally joined the Staffordshire County force in 1917, as a boy clerk. He had been promoted to sergeant in 1939.

Mr A H Furnival, a member of the Watch Committee, suggested that in future a sub committee of the Watch Committee be set up to confer with the Chief Constable on matters regarding promotion, a practice which was already popular in some forces, including Stoke-on-Trent. The Town Clerk was totally opposed to the idea and said, *"If the Chief Constable is not capable of making his own promotions then he is not capable of being the Chief Constable. I think that promotions through a committee would tend to lead to indiscipline within the force."*

Five members of the Police Reserve had retired during the previous year, all due to ill health. All were former policemen who had been called back into service in 1939.

Tenders for supplying uniforms for the Special and Regular Constabulary were requested and the committee decided against accepting the two lowest tenders as they felt that the cloth was of inferior quality. The tender was awarded to the local Enderley Mills once again.

The Chief Constable issued his annual report at the close of the year with the following figures:

	1943	**1944**
Indictable offences	324	563
Non-indictable offences	636	446
Juvenile offences	151	207
Road accidents	174 - 5 fatal.	
	(of which children 158 - 3 fatal)	

Stray Dogs: Seized: 334. Claimed: 66. Sold: 39. Destroyed: 151
Retained by finder: 78
Property found: Claimed: 747. Returned to finder: 153.
Lost children   **41 returned to parents.**

Parade of Regular and Special Constables Before HM Inspector de Coke 1945

Colonel J de Coke CMG, CVO, CBE, HM Inspector of Constabulary, inspected a parade of Regular and Special constables of the force in March. This was the first full inspection of the force since the outbreak of war.

Now that the war was nearing its end, the Watch Committee began to consider the housing of its policemen after the cessation of hostilities. The building of 26 houses on land in Whitmore Road and Talke Road was proposed, and some, but not all of these houses were built.

General Election

June saw a General Election, which necessitated extra duty for a large number of the Borough's undermanned police force. Most of the officers were on duty from 7am to 10pm. Each officer was paid 8/- for the extra hours worked.

The Watch Committee was asked by the Home Office to release the Chief Constable, Mr Jackson on a temporary basis to take up the position of Commandant of the newly opened District Training Centre at Ryton on Dunsmoor in Warwickshire. Mr Jackson was to remain at Ryton from May to December 1945. During his absence, Chief Inspector Lewis was in charge of the force, for which he was granted a non-pensionable allowance of £100 per annum.

Road Safety lectures were instituted for school children and Sergeant H Jones was instructed to visit all the schools in the Borough.

In his annual report for 1945, the Chief Constable refers to the theft of bicycles, which had become a major problem in the Borough.

HMI Parade and Inspection 1945

left to right:
Sgt. 6. L T H Pullman, 7. George Swettenham, 9. Alan Williams, 8. C W Naylor, 5. Frank Norcup, 3. G A Rutter, 2. I R Gogbill HMI Colonel J de F Coke CMG CVO CBE, Chief Constable G S Jackson, Chief Inspector E Lewis, The Mayor, Mr Ramsbottom.

**Strength of Force
1945**

On 17th July 1945, the strength of the Borough force is shown as follows:

Regular Police officers	41
First Police Reserves	3
Police War Reserves	10
Women Police Auxiliary	6
Total	60
Authorised strength	75

Nineteen members of the force were still serving in the Armed Forces. September saw the return of PCs Phillips, Chapman, Leak, Milburn, Lester, Moore, Henshall, Trigg, and Pritchard. All constables returning from the armed forces were sent on a six weeks refresher course at one of the District Training Centres.

Opposition to the Police Bill which was due to go before Parliament, requesting the abolition of the 47 non-county borough forces in England and Wales was not surprisingly very strong in Newcastle. The Town Clerk, along with the newly elected Labour M P for the Borough, headed a deputation to the Home Office.

In November, the blast wall, which had been erected in 1941, was removed from outside the Police Station. Six members of the Police War Reserve were released from their duties on 31st December 1945.

With Peace in Europe most of the auxiliary policemen returned to their pre-war occupations and the regular policemen returned to the force.

**Serious Death Toll
on the Borough's
Roads
1946**

In February the Chief Constable reported that 51 people had been killed on roads within the Borough since the outbreak of war in 1939.

The Women's Auxiliary Police Corps was disbanded on the 31st March 1946 but Mr Jackson suggested that three of the auxiliary police women be employed as civilian clerks.

Mr John Mack MP Fights for Borough Force Survival 1946

In February the MP for Newcastle, Mr John Mack, accompanied by the Town Clerk and along with the MPs for Luton and Chesterfield, met the Home Secretary to inform him of the opposition towards the Police Bill. They also asked if it would be possible to make Chesterfield, Luton and Newcastle-under-Lyme exempted districts, as they were under the Education Act. The deputation pointed out to the Home Secretary that it was unfair that these non-county borough forces were to be amalgamated but county borough forces like Chester*, Dewsbury and Wakefield, which were numerically smaller in strength, were allowed to remain. But all this was to no avail.

*Chester was amalgamated in 1949.

OBE Honour for Chief Constable

The Chief Constable Mr Jackson was awarded the OBE in the 1946 King's birthday honours. A short time later Mr Jackson tendered his resignation to the Watch Committee. He was to take up an appointment as the Chief Constable of Coventry City Police with effect from 1st November 1946.

Due to the impending amalgamation of the force, the Home Office refused to appoint another Chief Constable. Chief Inspector Lewis, who was the Deputy Chief Constable, had informed the Watch Committee that he intended to retire on 31st December. This left the Watch Committee with a dilemma on their hands. Eventually they managed to persuade Chief Inspector Lewis to stay until 31st March 1947. Mr Lewis had tried to retire in 1943, but his request had been refused due to the prevailing war conditions. When he did finally retire he had completed thirty seven and a half years of service.

The force was inspected for the last time on 8th October 1946 by Major MJ Egan OBE, H M Inspector of Constabulary.

On 22nd December 1946, John Willie Rimmington was sworn in before the Borough Magistrates. He was the last person to join the Newcastle-under-Lyme Borough Police. Since the appointment of Isaac Cottrill in 1834 to the appointment of John Willie Rimmington 112 years later, the policemen of the Borough must have worn out quite a lot of boot leather walking the streets of the

Newcastle Borough Police Force was inspected yesterday by HM Inspector of Constabulary, Colonel J de Coke CMG, CVO, CBE, seen in this picture with the Mayor, Alderman Mr J H Ramsbotham, in the ranks of the Special Constabulary, enjoying a joke with Mr G Kemp. Mr Kemp is High Constable of Newcastle and also serves as a special constable.

NEWCASTLE TO COVENTRY

18.9.46

Coventry Watch Committee this afternoon appointed Mr G S Jackson, Chief Constable of Newcastle-under-Lyme, to be Chief Constable of Coventry in succession to Captain S A Hector, who retires at the end of next month. Mr Jackson was chosen from a short list of seven candidates.

POLICE INSPECTION - Major M J Egan OBE, accompanied by the Mayor of Newcastle, Alderman F T Brent and the Chief Constable, Mr G S Jackson, inspecting the Mobile Unit during today's inspection of the Newcastle Borough Police at Cross Heath. The parade was in the charge of the Deputy Chief Constable, Mr F Lewis, who was complimented by Major Egan on the standard of turn-out.

town!

At the end of the year, the following items of cast-off clothing were purchased by the Castle Hotel; six jackets and six pairs of trousers, total cost; £13.10s.0d. It is not known for what purpose the hotel purchased these garments!

Force's Proud War Record

By November, the Acting Chief Constable was able to report that all the members had returned from War Service. Altogether, twenty men had served in the armed forces: 2 in the Royal Navy; 2 in the Royal marines; 4 in the RAF, and 12 in the Army. 17 of these men had returned to the police force. PC Price had resigned to go into business, PC Gibson had been offered a permanent commission in the RAF and PC Graig had made the supreme sacrifice (see appendices at end of book).

The Last days of the Borough Force 1947

With effect from New Year's day 1947, the Chief Constable's house at No 1, Priory Road, which had been vacant since Mr Jackson moved to Coventry, was let to the County and Superintendent CG Nixon took possession of the property.

The final meeting of the Watch Committee was held on Friday 14th March 1947 and was attended by Sir Herbert Patrick Hunter, Chief Constable of Staffordshire. In his address to the committee he said:

> *"This is not a grab by a large force against a small one. It did not come about like that, but through a provision of the government in the administration of the police service. I would also like to assure members of the Newcastle force that they would have a square deal within the County and every man would stand on his own merits."*

A number of questions were then asked by members of the committee, to which Sir Herbert replied. The committee thanked him for attending.

Newcastle Borough Force Merges with County Police March 1947

At midnight on 31st March, 1947, 112 years of service to the Borough ended when the Newcastle-under-Lyme Borough Police merged with the Staffordshire County Police. At 9.00am the following morning, Chief Inspector Lewis, the acting Chief Constable, formally handed over to Superintendent CG Nixon of the County force, the officers and documentation at the Borough Police Station, Merrial Street. The only visible sign, as far as the general public were concerned, was that their policemen were now wearing flat caps in place of helmets.

Members of the Regular and Special Constabulary taken with the Chief Constable Mr G S Jackson in 1946, prior to his departure for Plymouth to take up the post of Chief Constable of that City.
Author's collection

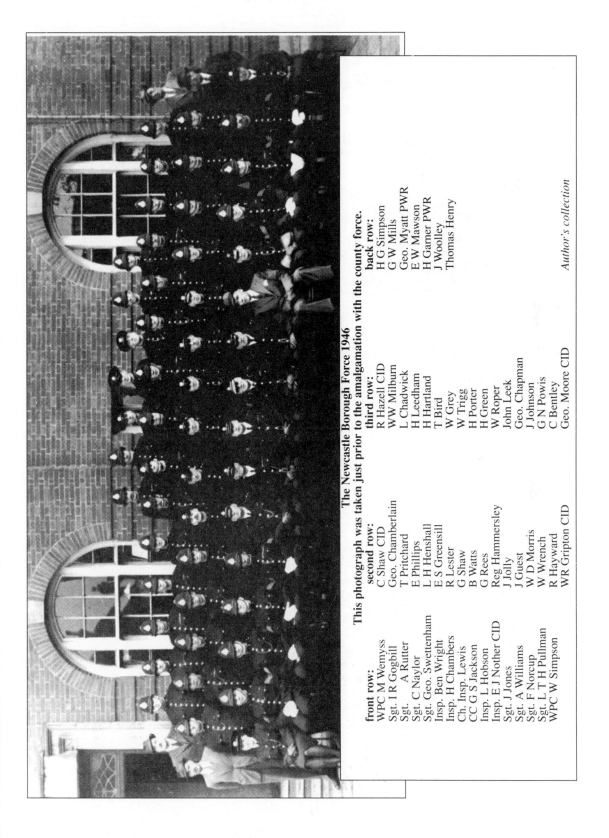

The Newcastle Borough Force 1946

This photograph was taken just prior to the amalgamation with the county force.

front row:
WPC M Wemyss
Sgt. I R Gogbill
Sgt.   A Rutter
Sgt. C Naylor
Sgt. Geo. Swettenham
Insp. Ben Wright
Insp. H Chambers
Ch. Insp. Lewis
CC G S Jackson
Insp. L Hobson
Insp. E J Nother CID
Sgt. J Jones
Sgt. A Williams
Sgt. F Norcup
Sgt. L T H Pullman
WPC W Simpson

second row:
C Shaw CID
Geo. Chamberlain
T Pritchard
E Phillips
L H Henshall
E S Greensill
R Lester
G Shaw
B Watts
G Rees
Reg Hammersley
J Jolly
J Guest
W D Morris
W Wrench
R Hayward
WR Gripton CID

third row:
R Hazell CID
WW Milburn
L Chadwick
H Leedham
H Hartland
T Bird
W Grey
W Trigg
H Porter
H Green
W Roper
John Leek
Geo. Chapman
J Johnson
G N Powis
C Bentley
Geo. Moore CID

back row:
H G Simpson
G W Mills
Geo. Myatt PWR
E W Mawson
H Garner PWR
J Woolley
Thomas Henry

Author's collection

1947 Police Change-Over: from today the Borough Forces of England and Wales lose their separate identities and become part of the constabularies of their respective counties. The picture shows the retiring acting Chief Constable of Newcastle, Mr E Lewis, handing over the charge-book at Newcastle Borough Police Office to Superintendent C G Nixon, who receives it on behalf of the Chief Constable of Staffordshire, Sir Hubert Hunter. *Sentinel*

Appendices
1 . Policewomen

In 1940, the Watch Committee asked the Chief Constable for his views on the appointment of police women to the force. Mr Bate's response was that there was no need for police women to be appointed at that time.

A few months later the committee received a memo from the Home Office relating to the appointment of police women auxiliaries. The Chief Constable told the committee that he had not altered his views.

In September 1941 the employment of police women in the Borough was still uppermost and a debate on the subject appears to have taken up most of the time at committee meetings, some members being in favour, some against. The Chief Constable himself was adamantly against the appointment of women. It was pointed out to Mr Bate that both Staffordshire County and Stoke-on-Trent City Police employed women. Mr Bate maintained that, in his opinion, police work was not women's work and there was plenty of useful war work that could provide employment for women. It was then suggested to the Chief Constable that he employ a number of Women Auxiliary Police Corps on telephone and office duties. To this, Mr Bate replied,

> *"I employ eleven members of the Police Reserve who are all retired police officers and are old servants of the state. They are able to do the work most efficiently. Some official work is most important and could not be entrusted to a woman."*

The Chief Constable was still firm in his refusal to appoint women to the Borough force, so much so that the Home Office sent along Colonel J de Coke CMG, CVO, CBE, HM Inspector of Constabulary, to discuss the matter with Mr Bate. At the end of the year, two members of the Women's Auxiliary Police were appointed. They were Miss Lewis and Miss Lawton and their appointment released two men for outside duties.

The Home Office later sent a circular to all police forces referring to the appointment of regular full time police women and on 25th May 1944, Mrs Ruby May Henshall was sworn in as Newcastle's first full time police woman. She had previously been a member of the WAPC and was the wife of PC Henshall. She resigned from the force eighteen months later, when her husband returned from war service.

On 31st March 1945, there were six members of the Women Auxiliary Police Corps employed by the Borough.
At a Watch Committee meeting held in January 1946, the Chief Constable Mr G S Jackson made the following statement to the committee,

"In consequence of the experience gained, I am pleased to say that police women are now an integrated part of the force and in view of this I ask the committee's approval to the appointment of three regular police women".

Mr Jackson's views were certainly different from those of his predecessor. In April 1946, Miss W Simpson and Miss M Wemyss, both members of the WAPC, were appointed as regular police women. A month later they were joined by Miss Jean Rawsthorne.

2 . Motor Transport

It would appear that the first motor vehicle owned and operated by the Borough police force was an old army ambulance purchased secondhand by the Council in 1919. By 1926, when it was finally replaced, it had made 150 journeys and travelled a total of 892 miles in that one year.

In 1923, the Watch Committee decided that in future the police would be responsible for running the ambulance, instead of the fire brigade, who had been operating it up to that time. The Committee thought that this would improve the efficiency of the ambulance in attending street accidents and emergency calls. Any change must have been one for the better, since at that time there were no full time firemen employed in the Town.

Less than twelve months later, the Chief Constable was reporting to the Committee that he had had the ambulance examined by a competent vehicle examiner, who had stated that it was in a dangerous condition and and should be taken out of use until all the faults he had listed were attended to. The repairs were carried out at a cost of £25.

In 1926 Mr Forster again reported to the Watch Committee on the condition of the ambulance. He said, *"I have had the ambulance examined again and the examiner has condemned it as unfit to be on the road, and in view of this report I have taken it out of use. I have, however, made arrangements with with the Chief Constable of Stoke-on-Trent to have the service of one of their ambulances to cover Newcastle, should the need arise."*

The Council contacted the British Red Cross Society as a matter of urgency and the Society presented an ambulance to the Borough. This ambulance appears to have been a gift to the Town as there is no record of it having been paid for by the Borough. The Red Cross were allowed to have use of this ambulance when required. At a meeting of the Watch Committee, held in 1928, the Mayor, Councillor Berrisford, the Chief Constable Mr W Forster

and Sir William VSG Goodwin made the following statement: *"We are the trustees of a fund which has now reached a total of £800 and with which we intend to purchase an ambulance for the use of the town and its people. The cost of the ambulance, however, is £851.1s.11d. The Council has, therefore, agreed to pay the balance of £51.1s.11d."*

The Watch Committee then took over custody and management of the new ambulance.

In 1934 the Chief Constable, Mr Lowe reported to the Watch Committee about the use of the ambulance by people from outside the Borough. Mr Lowe said that twice during the last month the police ambulance had been called out to attend incidents in the Biddulph area: *"When the ambulance attends a call in that area it means that two men are away from the Borough for approximately two hours. The Council have therefore instructed the Biddulph Authorities to make alternative arrangements with St John's."*

The Police Ambulance that had been in use for nine years, was replaced in 1937 by a new Daimler, purchased from Hanley Garage Ltd. at a cost of £704.10s.0d plus the old ambulance in part exchange. The new ambulance was fitted with a reconditioned engine in 1943, at a cost of £85. A Novax Resuscitation outfit was also purchased at a cost of £20, to be carried on the ambulance.
At this time the Chief Constable also requested the Council to upgrade the rates charged to persons using the ambulance. In future they would be charged 10/6d per turn out for journeys within the Borough. This would also include journeys to the City General Hospital and North Staffordshire Royal Infirmary, both situated in the City of Stoke-on-Trent. Persons using the ambulance outside the Borough were to pay 10/6d call out plus 1/6d per mile or part mile.

The force purchased their first traffic patrol car in 1931. It was an Austin 12hp and cost £275. This car was replaced two years later by a 16hp Austin and a Royal Enfield Motor Cycle Combination

at a total cost of £410.3s.0d, plus the old car in part exchange.
The car, along with the ambulance, was kept in a garage at the
premises of G T Bagguley Ltd, Printers, of High Street, for which
the Council paid a rent of £13 per annum, since there was no
garage accommodation at the old Police Station. Two years later
electric heaters were installed in the garage.

In 1935, two 10hp Hillman saloon cars were purchased for patrol
purposes. The old Austin which had been in use for the past two
years was taken in part exchange for the new vehicles. At the close
of 1935 the force possessed the following motor vehicles:

2 Hillman Patrol cars
1 Royal Enfield Motor Cycle Combination
1 Humber car for the use of the Chief Constable
1 Ambulance

The two Hillman Patrol cars were replaced in 1937 by two 10hp
Hillman Minx De Luxe saloon, the old cars being given in part
exchange.
It was suggested by a member of the Watch Committee that in
future the police cars be replaced annually, thus avoiding excess
depreciation and maintenance costs. This suggestion was
approved.
A petrol pump and a 500 gallon storage tank were installed at the
new police station and in 1938, the motor cycle combination,
which had been in use since 1933, was replaced by a 10hp
Commer Utility van which cost £171 plus the combination in part
exchange.
In the following year, the Chief Constable's official car, which had
been in use for the past seven years, was replaced by a new 1939
model 16hp Humber saloon.

At the beginning of 1940, both patrol cars were fitted with public
address systems and two second hand motor cycles were
purchased and added to the growing fleet. Wireless was installed
in the patrol cars in 1941. One of the Hillman cars and the
Commer Utility van were exchanged and replaced by two new
cars.

PC Reg Lester with Patrol Car 1946. *Ex-Superintendent Lester*

PC Reg Lester. Motor Patrol with Motor Cycle 1946.   *Ex-Superintendent Lester*

Motor Patrol Vehicles, 1946   *Staffordshire Police*

PC Reg Lester with Utility Van 1946.   *Ex-Superintendent Lester*

A new Ford Utility van was purchased in November 1944, at a cost of £341.5s.0d. Two new Austin 10hp saloon cars were purchased in 1945 to replace two of the patrol cars.

At this time, the main A34 trunk road (from Winchester to Preston) passed right through the centre of the town. In view of this the Chief Constable decided to modernise the Road Patrol Section. An MG TC 11hp sports car was purchased at a cost of £479.18s.4d. The main function if this vehicle was to patrol the trunk road, and for the first time officers attached to the section were issued with breeches and leather leggings. By this time most of the cars in use by the Borough force were fitted with two way radio.

At the time of the amalgamation in 1947, the force was in possession of the following vehicles, which were handed over to the County:

1 Chief Constable's staff car
3 Patrol cars
2 CID cars
1 Utility van
2 Motor cycles
1 Ambulance.

3 . The Special Constabulary

The first report of Special Constables being used in the Borough would appear to have been in 1842, during the Chartist Riots, when about 800 men were sworn in.

A letter received from the Home Office in October 1911, requested all police forces to form a Special Reserve. The Chief Constable informed the Watch Committee that he intended to get a list of about forty men who would be willing to serve as special constables in the Borough, should the need arise. In October of the following year, the Chief Constable was able to tell the Watch Committee that he had the names of 21 loyal gentlemen who were willing to serve. They had to wait almost three years before their services were required.

During the First World War, in 1915, the Chief Constable had a number of notices printed and displayed in various locations around the town, asking for men not eligible for military service due to age to become special constables in the Borough force. By the beginning of November, 70 men had come forward. They included Alderman Emery, the Rev J W Dunn, Rev A Sinker, Rev J G Hamlet and Rev J K Powell. By the end of the month, the Chief Constable had 90 specials and was able to report that the men were working satisfactorily, each man only being required to perform four hours patrolling per fortnight. They were able to choose their own nights of duty and also with whom they would share their patrol duty.

The Specials were each issued with an armlet and an aluminium number plate. Staff and handcuffs were available at the police office if required. They had to wait another five months before they were issued with uniform caps at a cost of 4/6d, which they were expected to pay for themselves!

During the Great War, members of the special constabulary also found time to organise a concert party which managed to raise, in 1918, £241.9s.0d, all of which was handed over to charities.

In November 1921, the Mayor, Councillor Whitfield, presented Long Service medals to members of the special constabulary who had served during the war.

During the General Strike in 1926 a large number of special constables were sworn in, but their services were not needed.

By September 1938, Mr Bate was able to report to the Watch Committee that the strength of the special constabulary was now 100 men. All performed duty in the town on Sunday and they performed it in the most exemplary manner. At the Chief Constable's request the committee ordered 110 special constabulary lapel badges. Five months later 200 armlets were purchased for the use of the special constabulary at a cost of 1/8d each.

In May 1939 the Chief Constable was authorised to purchase complete uniforms for 75 Specials. Each man would receive a cap, one pair of trousers, one serge jacket and one overcoat. 120 whistles and 120 truncheons were also bought. Six months later they were issued with waterproof coats. The newer members of the constabulary were issued with a loose lining to wear under their waterproof coats, instead of a greatcoat. In June 1942 the Chief Constable was authorised to obtain a greatcoat for each special constable who was not already in possession of one.

King's Theatre,
NEWCASTLE. STAFFS.
(By kind permission of F. W. Pendleton, Esq.)

Programme Souvenir
OF THE
Special Constables'
Charity Efforts

Grand Entertainment
Friday, 28th March, 1919,
IN AID OF THE POLICE ORPHANAGE.

UNDER THE DISTINGUISHED PATRONAGE OF
His Worship the Mayor and Mayoress,
the Corporation, and the Committee of the Mayor's Charities'
Funds of the Borough of Newcastle-under-Lyme.

No tenders appear to have been placed for uniform during the war years. All uniform was purchased from the Enderley Mills, which were and still are a local firm manufacturing uniform clothing.

Forty five members of the special constabulary were awarded long service medals in January 1943. The Chief Constable was able to report at the presentation that the special constabulary was operating in a most efficient manner. Most members were working four hour shift in the evening, either from 6pm -10pm or 8pm to 12 midnight. They also covered the town on Sundays in shifts, from 6am to 10pm. They were also expected to turn out when the alert was sounded. By this time, Mr Bate was able to report that each man was in possession of a complete uniform, including raincoat and greatcoat. Before the year was out each man was also issued with a pair of waterproof leggings. A new pair of trousers was also issued to each Special upon request.

On the recommendation of the Chief Constable, Mr George Douglas was appointed the Commandant of the Special Constabulary in February 1943. Mr Jackson was authorised to purchase a suitable uniform for him. Mr Douglas left the district in October 1945, having only served as Commandant for eighteen months. He was replaced by Mr Reg Butterworth. At a farewell evening for Mr Douglas, the Chief Constable said that since 1937, the number of men who had served in the Town's special constabulary was 212. There were 70 men still serving at that period. Since the outbreak of war most of the men had performed something in the order of 2,000 hours of duty and 16% had worked up to 3,000 hours. Mr Douglas said that the Specials had had to do more than had originally been anticipated, but somehow they had managed. Seventy waterproof capes were ordered for the use of the special constabulary at this time.

The following letter appeared in the local newspaper in March 1945:

> *The Newcastle Special Constabulary is now numerically under strength and it occurred to me that there might be a number of fit men who, through recent relaxation in some of the voluntary part time organi-*

THE BOROUGH MEN

sations, are now free to undertake voluntary police work.

I know that the volunteer spirit is as strong as ever it was, but I feel that it is not generally understood that relaxation in the Home Guard and Civil defence duties does not by any means imply a corresponding relaxation in police duties.

Police work must go on all the time, night and day, summer and winter, war or peace, yet it is difficult in these days, through so many regular policemen being away at war to give the public that supervisory service to which it is justly entitled.

The Specials have helped magnificently, but as I say, we are rather short of them. I wonder if you would help by drawing attention to these facts and invite anyone who would like to join the Specials to get in touch with me at the Borough Police Headquarters at Newcastle.

Yours faithfully,
George S Jackson
Chief Constable
Newcastle-under-Lyme

The special constabulary were released from their obligations in November 1945, but the Chief Constable were able to inform the Watch Committee that only one man had resigned. In 1945 the Specials worked 20,235 hours of duty and three of them, namely SCs Crick, Kemp and Riddell, along with P W R Butters, were to receive a commendation from the Watch Committee for the part they played in dealing with a disturbance in the town centre.

Although members of the special constabulary were very busy during the war years, they did manage to find time, together with a few members of the regular force, to organise a concert party, the proceeds of which were handed over to charity. The concert party still continued to be produced after the Borough force became absorbed into the County.

Chief Constables of Newcastle-under-Lyme Police.

1834 - 1849	Mr Isaac Cottrill
1850 - 1855	Mr John Thomas Blood
1855 - 1857	Mr Charles Barnes
1857 - 1861	Mr Charles Booth
1861 - 1866	Mr John Williams
1866 - 1870	Mr Stanford Alexander
1870 - 1878	Mr Walter Jones
1878 - 1881	Mr Charles Blyth
1881 - 1891	Mr Frederick Dutton
1891 - 1898	Mr George Taylor
1898 - 1901	Mr John Stirling
1901 - 1903	Mr Alfred H Richardson
1903 - 1912	Mr George Ingram
1912 - 1932	Mr William Forster
1932 - 1936	Mr George Sidney Lowe
1936 - 1943	Mr Wesley Bate
1943 - 1946	Mr George Spencer Jackson O.B.E.
1946 - 1947	Mr Ernest Lewis Acting Chief Constable

William Forster.

CHIEF CONSTABLE,
NEWCASTLE, STAFFS.

Roll of Honour

Members of the Newcastle-under-Lyme Borough Police Killed on Military or Police Service

P C Thomas Robinson Killed in action
July 1915.

P C Harry Royal Died from wounds,
14th March 1919

P C John Welch Killed by tramcar in Newcastle,
8th January 1915

S C Wilmot Sedgley Killed by enemy action,
16th January 1941

P C Robinson Craig Killed in action,
November 1943

Staffordshire County Police Officers who transferred to Newcastle-under-Lyme Borough Police on April 1st 1932

The following officers were transferred from the Staffordshire County Police, Newcastle Division, to the Newcastle-under-Lyme Borough Police when the Borough was enlarged on 1st April 1932:

Sergeant Ernest LEWIS
Sergeant Albert SKINNER
Sergeant Thomas SHIPLEY
Constable James CRAWFORD
Constable George CHAMBERLAIN
Constable Sidney Lawrence DURRENT
Constable Edwin S. GREENSILL
Constable John Henry JONES
Constable Charles LAWTON
Constable Geoffrey Wellstead MILLS
Constable Frederick MORRIS
Constable William Daniel MORRIS
Constable Edward Joseph NOTHER
Constable George Nelson POWIS
Constable Benjamin WRIGHT
Constable John William Norman WOOLLEY

Newcastle Borough Officers who transferred to Staffordshire County Police on 1st April 1947.

RANK	NAME	DATE APPOINTED
T/Ch.Insp	Leonard HOBSON	15.1.19
Insp	Harry CHAMBERS	20.1.19
Det. Insp	*Edward Joseph NOTHER	20.10.20
Insp	*Benjamin WRIGHT	10.1.17
T/Insp	*John Henry JONES	2.3.25
Sergeant 49	William ALLEN	21.1.23
Sergeant 2	Invictor Rex COGBILL	1.4.32
Sergeant.8	Clarence William NAYLOR	11.9.23
Sergeant.35	Frank NORCUP	1.11.24
Sergeant.26	Leslie T H PULLMAN	1.4.32
Sergeant.13	George Arthur RUTTER	19.10.25
T/Sergeant.44	Leonard B CHADWICK	18.10.27
T/Sergeant.78	Reg A HAMMERSLEY	13.8.39
PC 216	Thomas George R BIRD	21.1.32
PC 761	Clifford BENTLEY	21.5.39
PC 543	*George CHAMBERLAIN	27.2.26
PC 454	George Hy CHAPMAN	2.1.38
DC 765	David George COOPER	1.4.32
PC 10	William Edward DUNN	10.5.25
PC 769	William GRAY	1.5.35
PC 530	Henry GREEN	19.2.39
DC 135	William R GRIPTON	15.1.28
PC 548	*Edwin S GREENSILL	22.2.30
PC 234	James GUEST	2.12.27
PC 322	Harry HARTLAND	14.4.46
PC 390	Robert William HAYWARD	28.4.46
DC 327	Raymond HAZELL	2.3.33
PC 150	Thomas J HENRY	26.5.46
PC 249	Leonard H HENSHALL	28.8.36
PC 759	JW Clifford W HUGHES	10.5.39
PC 229	Harry F J JOLLY	1.4.32
PC 40	John JOHNSTON	5.5.46
PC 763	Harry W KENNEDY	13.8.39
PC 526	John Alfred LEAK	26.12.37
PC 760	Harry LEEDHAM	4.5 39
PC 142	Charles Reginald LESTER	3.10.37
PC 762	Edward Norman MAWSON	2.10.27
PC 30	Robert McINTYRE	15. 9.46
PC 438	William W MILBURN	10.2. 39
DC205	George Harold MOORE	6.8 .35
PC 768	*Frederick MORRIS	30.6. 23
PC 244	*William Daniel MORRIS	15.12.26
PC 767	*Geoffrey Wellstead MILLS	27.9.30
PC 518	John Henry F MUMFORD	1.1.35
PC 755	Eric D PHILLIPS	1.7.38

RANK	NAME	DATE APPOINTED
PC 372	Harold H PORTER	17.4.38
PC 147	* George Nelson POWIS	26.10.29
PC 756	Thomas R PRITCHARD	14.8.38
PC 311	George Dennis REES	18.10.29
PC 121	John Willie RIMMINGTON	22.12.46
PC 432	W G M Bruce ROBB	1.4.32
PC 282	William ROPER	1.4.32
PC 766	Huntley G SIMPSON	28.5.46
PC 533	George N SHAW	1.4.32
DC 757	Cyril SHAW	29.8.37
PC 266	Joseph B THORNTHWAITE	1.4.32
PC 758	William TRIGG	1.5.39
PC 117	Samuel Robert WATTS	12.11.27
PC 636	*John W.N WOOLLEY	24.3.19
PC 319	William B WRENCH	24.3.46
WPC 23	Winifred SIMPSON	5.2.45
WPC 24	Marjorie WEMYSS	2.3.45
WPC 25	Jean RAWSTHORNE	5.5.46
P(WR)C	George MYATT	War Reserve
P(WR)C	Harry GARNER	War Reserve

* Indicates original members of the Staffordshire County Police taken into Newcastle Borough Police on 1st April 1932.

Insignia of the Borough Force

As far as can be established the first insignia worn on head dress by the Newcastle-under-Lyme Borough police appears to be the shako badge. This comprised of a small uncrowned oak wreath with the official seal of the Newcastle borough in the centre. The badge was of white metal, but also exists in black, presumably for night duty. It was worn on the shako by sergeants and constables, then later on caps, until the amalgamation of the force in 1947. From the mid 1930's these badges were chromed.

Officers wore an embroidered version of the seal until the 1930's, when the standard blue enamelled officer's cap badge was adopted, which bore the Borough seal in the centre.

The first helmet plates worn by the force consisted of a large star surmounted by the Victorian crown. Within the centre of the star was the Borough seal, surrounded by the force title, 'Borough of Newcastle-under-Lyme Police'.

After the death of Queen Victoria, like most police forces the Borough force had the Victorian crown removed and replaced with a King's crown. This badge remained in use until the amalgamation in 1947. It was also chromed in the mid 1930's.

Special constables wore the cap badge as described above, when in uniform. The special constables' lapel badge comprised a blue enamelled oval badge bearing the Borough seal, surrounded by the words 'Borough of Newcastle-under-Lyme Special Constable'.

Collar badges were in the form of the small castle which appears in the Borough seal.

Uniform belts were worn with ornate buckles until about 1932. There appear to have been two designs. The first pattern consisted of the Borough seal surrounded by an oak wreath, the second bears the Borough seal surrounded by the words 'Borough of Newcastle-under-Lyme Police'.

Helmet Plates of Newcastle Borough Force. Left: pre-1901, with the Victorian Crown. Right: 1901 - 47 with the King's Crown.

Belt Buckle, possibly the first pattern.   *Photography by John Lightfoot*

The Seal of the Borough of Newcastle

The seal of the Borough of Newcastle-under-Lyme dates from the thirteenth century and contains a representation of the 'new castle' which was built in the twelfth century. On the central tower are two men, one holding an axe and the other blowing a horn. From the battlements hang three shields, the centre one bearing the three lions of England - a reference to Henry III. The second shield displays a lion rampant within a border charged with roundels, for Edmund, Earl of Cornwall, and the third bears the three wheat sheaves of the Earldom of Cheshire, which was held, in the reign of Henry III, by his son prince Edward.

Top: Cap badge, first issued in 1868 for use on the shako. This badge was issued in black, white metal and chrome.
Middle: Special Constable's off duty lapel badge.
Bottom: Officer's cap badge, first issued 1935
Side: Epaulette badges.   *Author's collection*

The Coat of Arms
of
Newcastle under Lyme.

Scott Series No 525